Carol D. Mitchell

CAROL

MITCHELL

Your Rights Employment Guide

ALL RIGHTS RESERVED

International Standard Book Number CDMBOOKS

NON-EXCLUSIVE

CAROL DENISE MITCHELL
ISBN-13:978-1505343199
ISBN-10:1505343194

Vacaville ● California ● United States of America

Your Rights

Employment Guide

> The sale of this book without its cover is unauthorized. If you purchased this book without a cover, you should be aware that it was reported to the publisher as "unsold and destroyed." Neither the author nor the publisher received payment for the sale of this "stripped book." **Please note - this book was written in 2005. For current references of changing material dates and times - please use information provided in this guide - to update resources for future use always!**

This book is a work of non-fiction, but some names, characters, places and incidents are fictional and are products of the author's imagination or are used fictitiously. Any resemblance to actual events/locales or persons, living or dead is entirely coincidental.

CAROL MITCHELL BOOKS
Vacaville, Concord, California 95687 – 6068
Carol Denise Mitchell P/K/A CDM
All rights reserved, including the right to reproduce
this book or portions thereof in any form whatsoever.
For information, write to: cdmbooks@aol.com
Edited by: Carol Denise Mitchell

Carol D. Mitchell

TABLE OF CONTENTS

Chapter 01………..What Is an Employee   Page # 10

Chapter 02………..The Smart Page   Page # 12

Chapter 03………..The Professional You   Page # 17

Chapter 04………..From the Beginning   Page # 22

Chapter 05………..Sample Company Time Card Page # 27

Chapter 06………..Prevent Losing   Page # 30

Chapter 07………..Labor Law   Page # 35

Chapter 08………..Fired   Page # 45

Chapter 09………..The Resources Manager   Page # 54

Chapter 10………..Your Protected Rights   Page # 61

Chapter 11………..Sexual Harassment…   Page # 67

Chapter 12………..Sample Letters 1   Page # 79

Chapter 13………..50 Fastest Growing   Page # 86

Chapter 14………..Division of Labor Standards Page # 97

Chapter 15………..Workers Compensation   Page # 103

Chapter 16………..Cover Letters   Page # 128

Chapter 17………..The Cheat Sheet   Page # 140

Chapter 18………..Temporary Rights   Page # 169

Chapter 19………..The Five Star Superior You Page # 179

Chapter 20………..In the News   Page # 182

BIBLIOGRAPHY   Page # 198

Your Rights Employment Guide

DEDICATION PAGE

This book is dedicated to workers across America, the outstanding men and women in private, state, local, and federal agencies, often unknown and unseen whose earnest intendments are to serve employers well.

Special thanks to my brother Jerry Charles for encouraging me to do what compels me to help others.

Thanks to my beloved grandmother, Garthia Pierson, my mother, Tasceaie and my father Zebbie Charles. Also, thanks to my brothers and sisters and my children, Shuun and Daryle, Marie and Shakiyma.

In memory of Mamus, Mother, Daddy, Victor, Fuzzy, and Annie Davis. Your inspiring lives bring light to my soul. You are all missed. Last, but not least, thanks to American workers across the USA

Carol D. Mitchell

From the Author

Your Rights Are Important! My sincere incentive for writing this guide is to bring into being a much more level playing field for the employee in a rapidly changing and fluid modern working environment. The archetypal American worker goes to work to keep a roof over his/her head and to provide food on the table for their families. When they are hired to work for a company, few employees are told up front about <u>all</u> of their employment rights. Therefore, American workers are truly at the mercy of the employer, who can out wit and outlast the everyday working person. Reality proves that the everyday worker must learn the defenses they are going to need if their earnest work efforts and good intentions on a job go awry. While many employers have fancy law firms defending their interest; employees have few resources to fight back with, and they have even less time to do the research to carry it out. While the employer is fully aware of employment rights and the law, few employees know their rights. That is why I have written this handbook. This guide is specifically for the employee. For it is necessary in this highly technical society to have first-hand knowledge of what is needed for one to protect their own interest. Being smart in acquiring the right job means understanding the characteristics and qualifications that employers are looking for in you. A serious job candidate should treat the employment resume like it is the tailor-made suit or gown for their wedding. Fit it to meet distinct body measurements that will display your best attributes directly in calibration with the employer's requirements. When you are hired, be in step with what is going on with the employer. Understand your rights under Department of Labor employment law. Comprehend the many excellent choices you do have in choosing the employer that is right for you. Examine the list in this book of *"100 Best Companies to Work for in America,"* and see if one of the five largest temporary employment agencies listed in this guide is the right employer for you.

With that in mind, I have taken great measures in this book to observe the employer introspectively. I wanted to know why they keep paper trails, and what they do with them. Even more importantly than that, I wanted to know why they fire, how they fire, and how you could work towards keeping the job you love. When I unearthed answers that I felt were right for you, I then harnessed that well-regulated information and the employer's ubiquitous thinking about you from the reverse perspective to give to you, the employee. After reading

Your Rights
Employment Guide

this chief employee tool-guide, you will have at your fingertips information you will need to be treated fairly on your job.

Additionally, you will be set to get out into the job market professionally knowing what company to work for, and what to say on the interview to nail the job. Then, you will deliver to your employer exactly what is expected of you with precision knowledge, for after you read this guide, you will be informed.

Consequently, if you already have a job, you will have increased certainty in your ability to deliver to your company what your employer wants. Additionally, with your acquired wisdom you will have the ability to fight for your rights. Unfortunately, if it turns out that you have to wage warfare for your job; then you will have the basic tools to cogently wage a fierce and successful battle over whatever may be rightfully yours.

Remember that a good employee and a good employer generally want the same things. The employee wants to know what the company is about and how to become an integral part of the enterprise. The employer wants you to learn what they are about, be a team player, and produce. However, when employees are productive for a company they want to know that their genuine, efforts are appreciated in the workplace. Notwithstanding, the sad reality of this day is that many employees never get praise or the two simple words from their supervisors or managers that can make all the difference in the world towards continual commitment and productivity, and those words are "thank you." While employees are starving for this kind of affirmation from the employer; we live in a litigious society and employers know that some employees are smart enough to write kind gestures and inculpable praises down to use later if things at work go wrong. Consequently, employers are disinclined sometimes to give credit openly where it is due, thereby creating a lack of communication and understanding of the employee's remarkable accomplishments.

Sadly, it does not cost a company a dime to say kind words to individuals who are being productive. Saying, *"hey, just want to tell you to keep up the good work,"* can mean all the difference in the world to the individual who is hardworking and giving.

It is your right to know how to keep abreast of your employer. I encourage you to keep track

Carol D. Mitchell

of everything. My message to the employee is, *"write it down."* After all, you are trustworthy, and you have taken the time to effectively and accurately live up to the expectations of the employer. Imagine that you wanted to be challenged, so you ranked at the top of the scale for setting forth your visions towards the company's ongoing prosperity. Then you were unceremoniously fired. Say you were a victim of redundancy, and the employer told you that the position you molded, and worked so hard in had been discontinued.

Imagine a friend and former co-worker tells you that a recent college graduate Joe Blow, with less experience and education than you had was hired into your old job days after you were fired. If something like that happens to you *know your rights*[1]. Read this smart guide and use your good note taking to prove your previous contributions in the job that you lost. Know who to call and when to call them.

Discern and then understand what forms you need to fill out; and, how to fill them out properly. If you are in a union get immediate assistance. Read on and review a variety of resources and information that your boss does not want you to know. Be a better employee for the employer. And most importantly, be a better one for you!

---

[1] If you are forty years of age or older and you were replaced by someone who was younger than forty years of age, you may be a victim of age discrimination and protected under the Age Discrimination Employment Act (ADEA) as well as your State Anti-Discrimination law.

Your Rights

Employment Guide

"Democracy cannot work unless it is honored in the factory as well as the polling booth; men cannot be truly free in body and in spirit unless their freedom extends into the places where they earn their daily bread."

Senator Robert F. Wagner in 1935,
Upon offering his Bill that was to become
The Nation's Basic Labor Law.

Carol D. Mitchell

THE DISCLAIMER

The use of this guide is for readers who want easy access to personal and published information regarding employment rights. As more fully set forth in the terms of your using this guide, the data provided here is for general information purposes; it is not a determination of your legal rights nor your responsibilities under the law. I am not a lawyer, and none of the information contained in this guide is, or should be defined as, legal advice. I am not engaged in the practice of law, and no attorney-client relationship is being created. Any information communicated to any lawyer via this guide does not have the confidentiality protection of the attorney/client privilege. Laws do change often. This guide contains information that is current to date and the purpose of this guide is to provide you with information that will be illuminative. If you are seeking legal advice, find a qualified lawyer in your area. If you need help in finding a lawyer, call your local, county, state bar association, or check out the information below.

- National Employment Lawyers Association, (NELA) @ http://www.nela.org/home.cfm NELA is the largest and most effective plaintiff employment lawyer organization in the United States. The headquarters is located in San Francisco, California.
- Workplace Fairness at Http://www.workplacefairness.org. This is an excellent web-site for *lay* people to learn about their rights as employees and how to save or get their job back

Your Rights
Employment Guide

Chapter 1
What Is an Employee?

Generally, the definition of the word, "employee" has varying meanings. When it comes to you knowing what role "employee" in a company is be aware that you are an employee if a company hires you to perform a distinct form of labor or work. Your offering to a specific job and or industry has a lot to do with what job you were hired to do, and how your skills, and or education and experience match, and can positively influence ongoing residual profit for the company. Work titles cover a wide range of professional business from accountants to lawyers. With the recent boom in technology, some professional work titles are transcending conventional definition and are changing with trends. Some employees, *(depending on the work contract)*, are permanent and they receive a guaranteed wage. Others may be hired as temporary employees, contract employees, or as consultants.

WHAT IS EMPLOYMENT

Employment is a contract and or grouping between two parties, the *employer* and the *employee*. The employee is typically chosen via a competitive hiring process where other candidates are eliminated. This process may include but is not limited to:

- Filling out an employment application
- Interviewing with the hiring manager and or supervisor of the department
- Second, & sometimes third interviews with management level professionals

When hired the employee signs on with the employer. The newly hired person then services the employer in a mercantile setting giving suitable and congruous productivity to the hiring party with the intention of maintaining and or creating profits. The hired employee works in public, nonprofit and or private settings and then dispenses labor to the hiring entity or enterprise in return for a pre-specified amount of pay or wages. In the United States most employees are designated "at will." In this case, either the employer or employee can *(without fear of reprisal)* stop employment, at any time for any cause or simply for no reason.

Carol D. Mitchell

National Employment Lawyers Association, (NELA) @ http://www.nela.org/home.cfm

- NELA is the country's only professional organization that is exclusively comprised of lawyers who represent individual employees in cases involving employment discrimination and other employment-related matters. The headquarters is located in San Francisco, California.
- Workplace Fairness at http://www.workplacefairness.org. This is an excellent web-site for **lay** people to learn about their rights as employees and how to save or get their job back.

A FEW THINGS THE EMPLOYER MAY NOT WANT YOU TO KNOW

1. **The law period**

How to easily interpret difficult contracts/policy

2. **Where to go for help**

How to acquire immediate help resources to defend your interest

3. **The Paper Trail**

How they are tracking your *every* effort on the job

4. **The truth about the "Offer Letter"**

How it is a *legal and binding* contract of employment

5. **Title VII of the Civil Rights Act**

How it protects you against harassment, discrimination, etc.

6. **Age Discrimination, (ADEA)**

How you can fight after being fired over 40

7. **Who is in Charge**

How to contact *decision making executives* for resolve

8. **Workers Compensation Law**

They particularly do not want their insurance rates to go up

9. **How to fight for your rights**

For employers; the less you know about your rights, the better

Your Rights
Employment Guide

Chapter 2
The Smart Page

THE MOST IMPORTANT THINGS TO TAKE TO WORK

1. The *Smart Page Weekly hand-sheet*. In time of need - it will be your guiding light. You have already seen how bad the job market is. Now it is more important than ever to know your full-vested interest in your job. It's what people are calling an "Employer's" market. Individuals are going on anywhere from 3-5 interviews for just one job! If you have a job you need to keep it and here is how.

Write something on your sheet or diary every day. If you take public transportation to work, instead of reading the paper, write down events of the previous day. You will be glad at how useful this information can be. Even the most mundane and unimportant things today, could be your saving grace tomorrow!

WHY IT'S IMPORTANT TO WRITE THINGS DOWN

1. It's hard to lie about an exact date and or time
2. Pinning times and dates give you more credibility
3. Your memory can not always be relied upon
4. Facts can be sustained easier
5. It jogs your memory better

Carol D. Mitchell

HELP IS ON THE WAY

The employer is on your trail. Therefore, your Smart Page Weekly hand-sheet allows you to record your good work and write down areas where you want to grow and keep track of all of your special projects and your overtime hours in a neat way that you will invariably need later. With smart tips, handy charts, snappy letters, resumes and much more, this useful data guide, will spare you the overall trouble of worrying where to go to handle your business when it comes to your job and how to produce important facts. With your great attention to detail, save your job, and prove to your employer exactly how well you really have been doing it. Know how important government work web-sites will be if you need to file a claim for unemployment insurance, or whatever you need in your employment future. Check out your Smart Page Weekly hand-sheet below and download other forms easily using information provided for you at the following government links!

- U.S. Department of Labor, www.dol.gov
- U.S. Equal Employment Opportunity Commission www.eeoc.gov
- U.S. Department of Justice, www.usdoj.gov
- The Internal Revenue Service, www.irs.gov

Being able to access important help pages will save you the time of wondering where to go for information and where to get important forms. Many web pages allow you to download forms easily. Did you know that you can apply for Unemployment benefits on line? In California, there are few places, if any to go fill out unemployment forms. Now it's easier to download forms on the computer. Go online even, and complete an application that is processed more expeditiously! Even if your job is not threatened today, each employee should know what's out there for him or her in case they have to use these resources tomorrow. No employee can ever have too much information when it comes to implementing and exercising employment rights.

Your Rights

Employment Guide

THE WEEKLY HAND SHEET

				FIRST:	LAST:
	Name Here				
	Address Here				
	Telephone Here				City/State/Zip
	Cell/Mobile Here				
	E-mail/Website Here				
	Employment Information			<u>Smile</u> Notes	**PLACE OF EMPLOYMENT** **COMPANY NAME**
	Start Date\				**COMPANY ADDRESS**
	Position Title\				**COMPANY PHONE**
Weekly Work Track Record					Weekly Hand-sheet Work Comments
Monday	Date :	Y= OK	N=Not	Y	N
Tuesday	Date :	Y= OK	N=Not	Y	N
Wednesday	Date :	Y= OK	N=Not	Y	N

Carol D. Mitchell

				Y	N	
Thursday	Date :	Y= OK	N=N ot			
Friday	Date :	Y= OK	N=N ot	Y	N	
Saturday	Date :	Y= OK	N=N ot	Y	N	
Sunday	Date :	Y= OK	N=N ot	Y	N	
Project Day 1. Monday 2. Tuesday 3. Wednesday 4. Thursday 5. Friday		Project Name		Happy Notes		Detailed Comments

Overtime worked, explain in comments
Name of project worked on:
 	
Amount of time:
_____
Amount of time:
_____
Amount of time:
_____
						More comments on overtime:
						
						Approved by: _____
						    Date approved: _____
						
						Approved by: _____
						    Date approved: _____
						
						Approved by: _____
						    Date approved: _____

Your Rights

Employment Guide

MY After Work Weekly WORKSHEET

Date/In/Out to be checked ☐				Daily Time	Hourly report. Hours worked, And recorded for personal records.
Breaks	In	Out	Lunchtime		COMMENTS
				8:00	
				9:00	
				10.00	
				11:00	
				12:00	
				1:00	
				2:00	
				3:00	
				4:00	
				5:00	
					---------- Daily Work & Time Report ----------

Carol D. Mitchell

Chapter 3
The Professional You

THE PROFESSIONAL YOU

By now you know that if the employer threatens your livelihood - you are going to wage a battle for your rights. Before then, in order to ensure that you are on the right footing with the employer, you must be serious about doing your part fully when it comes to your job.

At work, be courteous, be polite, be considerate, be concerned, be respectful, and be quietly professional at all times. Give the employer a chance to be good to you!

- Don't be the company clown
- Do buy a thesaurus; use it!
- Don't get drunk at work, or luncheons
- Do finish projects completely
- Don't give gifts to the boss
- Do influence others positively
- Don't *clown* the boss in public
- Do offer solutions to problems
- Don't address anyone as, "hey you"
- Do think, then speak
- Don't lose your strong work ethic
- Do exercise savvy Internet skills
- Don't ever be late for work
- Do the nice thing to all

ON OUR HONOR WE DO OUR DUTY

Most employees arrive to work ready to give 100% to the employer, as they should. As good workers, we honor the employer by giving our complete dedication, our promised dependability and full obligation to carry out our job in the way that we are hired for. Many of

Your Rights
Employment Guide

us are not college graduates and some of us are. The majority of us have a commendable work ethic. We come to work eager and prepared to do the job.

We ask the right questions in turn we receive the right answers towards a long future with a great company. When things don't turn out right at work, there are many factors to be considered other than that I am not doing my job. Unfortunately, many employees who go to work to serve are often victimized, or cheated when things at work go awry. Employees in general have little time to endure a long process of fighting for benefits, lost wages or other compensation that are due to them when the work relationship dies. Therefore, employees will march off the job leaving behind earned overtime payments, worker's compensation benefits, unemployment insurance benefits and unresolved discrimination and harassment claims.

While you are fed up your employer is aware that laws are ever changing. Your well-informed employer is therefore keeping your money in the bank. They are drawing interest on your funds banking that you will move on with your life, rather than claim from them what is rightfully yours. Moreover, behind your back, the employer has an impressive paper trail on you. So, why not start-off with the Company by giving the employer exactly what they are looking for.

Carol D. Mitchell

KNOW AND DO WHAT THE EMPLOYER WANTS

According to surveys, employers seek the following qualifications in recent college graduates. This list can serve as a guide for those who want to sell themselves for what employers say they want.

Work Experience	Computer Work	Problem Solving Skills
If you are applying for a job as a receptionist, you may have had some skills in your early past that helps you build experience for that job. For instance, if you worked in your high-school administrative office, use that towards experience on your application to be a receptionist.	With the increased demand for IT professionals and jobs alike, computer experience is required for just about every job in business, education and government agencies. If you have a computer at home and you make flyers, or write down notes; use that experience on your job application.	When the employer is trying to ascertain your level of critical thinking, use clear and concise situations where your problem solving skills has tangibly offset what could have been a worse problem. Personal life experiences can help you build a resume in line with what the employer is looking for!

Your Rights

Employment Guide

DID YOU KNOW?

It is your right to:

- Refuse to work seven days straight (*unless your employer is exempt by law?*)
- Vote. Tip: (*Always give your employer notice.*) It is your right to vote!
- Take time off work to appear as a witness. Tip: (*Give your employer notice.*)
- Serve on a jury. (Yes, give *them* notice.)
- File for bankruptcy and not be fired!

Intentional or not, many supervisors, and or managers are not fully aware how to make sure that all of your rights are protected and that includes hiring without illegal discrimination. Therefore, it is up to you, the employee, to embrace the laws that protect you in the interview, and then in the workplace. Be ready, be equipped and be smart when it comes to your employment rights.

Communication Skills	Leadership Experiences	Dependability
In the professional work environment, nothing says it more than a person who speaks well and gets along well with people from diverse, and all cultures. Use your strong writing, research and public speaking experience to clarify on your application your strong communication skills.	Many of us have participated in activities that have honed our developmental and social skills, and we discount them because we feel that they are not job related. Consider using all applicable skills for the job, you are interested in applying.	Whether you are a college graduate or not, you probably know how important it is to show up on a job every day at the right time. Prove to your employer that you know the importance of being a dependable employee that they can rely on to be on time and at work every day.

Carol D. Mitchell

THINGS TO REMEMBER

- ☐ Use all relevant work and life skills towards getting the job
- ☐ Never, ever lie on your application or job resume
- ☐ Know your strengths and weaknesses
- ☐ In interviews, downplay weak points, play up strengths
- ☐ Be positive. Speak well of others; be a problem solver
- ☐ Never, ever be late for work: (leave earlier to get there on time)

Your Rights
Employment Guide

Chapter 4
From the Beginning

From the beginning

When you seek out a company for employment, you are asking them to entrust you to be a part of an industry that many companies consider family. If you are hired, you are going to be at the business more than one quarter of the day. You are the greatest resource of the business because with your skills, work experience and education, you are valuable. The employer knows that managing people correctly can take up priceless production time. Therefore, to keep controversy to a minimum, the lawyers have given employers an employee blueprint on how to effectively hire and fire you. Beware!

☐ They are going to give you a ***Job Description***. They are going to imply, but not tell you that the job description clarifies your role <u>fully</u>. They use the job description to avoid mystification about your role, define the essential functions of the position, and to have a leg to stand on legally if you sue them later.

☐ They are going to provide you with a document generally termed an "***Employment Offer*** *or "Offer of Employment"*. This letter is designed with more structure than the Golden Gate Bridge. Lawyers advise companies to give you this letter before you start the job. They want you to read the letter and sign it. Once you have signed the employment letter and returned it to the employer, you have officially signed a *legal contract*, which in most cases will be careful not to provide you with a property interest in the position. If the employer does not tell you that there is a probationary period in the letter, they may have negated an important key regarding your employment rights.

☐ The ***Probationary period*** can be used as a tool to summarily fire you at any time during the specified time of probation. A usual feature of a probationary period is that the employer may end your employment without affording you a due process procedure that may be

Carol D. Mitchell

afforded to non-probationary employees. Usually a probationary period is ninety days. In most companies, employee's legal status is at will. Simply put, "at will" employees may be terminated for any legal reason at the discretion of the employer. The employer may fire the employee for anything or the employee may leave for any reason without giving notice to the employer.

However, to play it smart, they may simply fire you without cause saying that you did not pass the probationary period and unless they have violated your ***protected rights***, there is little you can do about an "at will" firing. Generally a private sector employee, who is not carried by a union, is considered to be "at will" under the law. Therefore, without a written employment contract, or prevailing enforceable verbal contract, an employer may without breaking the laws per se, fire an employee, so long as they do not breach a protected class or break the law. ***Remember:*** it is always wise to do your research, using the resources provided herein, and challenge an employer who fires you for no reason.

- Judges are keenly aware of the "at will" laws. They know the law allows employers to fire innocent people sometimes. Again, for probation to be sensible, and adequate, it has to be agreed upon between yourself and the employer before you start the job.

- ***References.*** **Employment Defense** Lawyers and other employer advocates believe that there are an increasing number of people providing false employment details and fake references to promote their bid for the job. *TIP:* They are telling the employer to confirm your references and to talk directly to past employers or they will use professional screening services to track down the truth. *Advice:* Be honest. Even if you had a bad relationship with a past employer, call them. Ask them to give you a start, and end date, of your last job on company letterhead. Tell them it is against the law to tell a future employer things about you that are not true. That way when you fill out an application for a new job, you have tangible proof from the Department of Human Resources that your dates are accurate. No company wants to risk a potential defamation lawsuit. Instead, your former company will be more than willing to give you a start and end date reference. You cannot always rely on friends or false references.

- **Employment Defense** Lawyers and other employer advocates are telling the employer to settle. If the employer has not done things right by you from the beginning, they dig themselves a hole. Let me be honest. There are unqualified people wearing big hats in

Your Rights
Employment Guide

companies that do not know how to be fair to employees. Unprofessional behavior and incompetence on the part of the employer can cost time and money regardless whether the company at issue is right or wrong.

- Good and fair employment practices are vital to a serious business. Good employment practice can reduce cost. Therefore, you can help your company maintain being a great employer by assuring yourself of the following:

- Follow the company rules
- Know your legal employee/employment rights
- Keep your own paper trail to match or better employer
- Stay calm, resolve work issues, try not to get fired
- Call your lawyer to read employment agreements, contracts

Special note regarding your pension & important U.S. Department of Labor facts
Resource: http://www.dol.gov/ebsa/Publications/protect_your_pension.html#section3

Finding Out About The Rules

Under federal law your pension plan is required to give you information about plan investments. The plan must automatically provide you with a summary of its finances for each year, or a written notice of your right to receive that summary. The summary is called a **summary annual report**, or SAR. In addition, if you ask for it in writing, you must be given a copy of the full annual report and financial statements that the plan files with the government. Plans covering 100 or more participants generally must use a **Form 5500** and plans covering less than 100 participants can use a simpler version called a **Form 5500-C/R**. The forms usually must be filed with the government within seven months after the end of the calendar year or other 12-month period your plan uses for financial reporting purposes.

Summary Annual Reports - If you are in a plan that files a Form 5500, the plan must give you a summary annual report (SAR) each year.

Ordinarily one to two pages long, the SAR summarizes information contained in the plan's

Carol D. Mitchell

more detailed Form 5500 financial statements, and will give you a sense of how well your pension plan's investments have performed. For example, it shows:

Whether the plan's investments have lost large amounts of money during a year;
The plan's total administrative expenses for the year;

A list of items that can alert you to questionable financial arrangements with individuals or organizations closely connected to the plan; and

If any money loaned by the plan has not been paid back on time.

If you have been with a company for a long time and they owe you a pension, check into it religiously. You are entitled to your pension. You earned this money through your dedicated service and if something is not right with your pension, then you should contact the U.S. Department of Labor's Pension and Welfare Benefit Administration (PWBA), for assistance at http://www.dol.gov/dol/topic/retirement/participantrights.htm

Your earnings are important to you. Did you know that the U.S. Department of Labor compiles Labor Statistics Data to keep assiduous track of your hours? Your employer takes keeping track of your hours seriously enough to provide this data (regularly) to the government. Below, see one example of who is working overtime and why you must keep track of *__your own personal time__* as attentively as they keep track of you!

From U.S. Department of Labor Bureau of Labor Statistics - www.bls.gov

Employment, Hours and Earnings from the Current Employment Statistics Survey (National)

Resource Information

http://www.dol.gov/dol/budget/2010/PDF/CBJ-2010-V1-04.pdf

TRAINING AND EMPLOYMENT SERVICES (A) [$283,051,000] *$229,160,000* for the dislocated workers assistance national reserve, of which [$71,051,000] *$17,160,000* shall be available for the period July 1, [2009] *2010* through June 30, [2010] *2011*, and of which $212,000,000 shall be available for the period October 1, [2009] *2010* through June 30, [2010: Provided, That up to $125,000,000 may be made available for Community-Based Job Training grants from funds reserved under section 132(a)(2)(A) of the WIA and shall be used to carry out such grants under section 171(d) of such Act, except that the 10 percent limitation otherwise applicable to the amount of funds that may be used to carry out section 171(d) shall not be applicable to funds used for Community-Based Job Training grants: Provided further,

Your Rights

Employment Guide

That funds provided to carry out section 132(a)(2)(A) of the WIA may be used to provide assistance to a State for State-wide or local use in order to address cases where there have been worker dislocations across multiple sectors or across multiple local areas and such workers remain dislocated; coordinate the State workforce development plan with emerging economic development needs; and train such eligible dislocated workers: Provided further, That funds provided to carry out section 171(d) of the WIA may be used for demonstration projects that provide assistance to new entrants in the workforce and incumbent workers] *2011*; (B) $52,758,000 for Native American programs, which shall be available for the period July 1, [2009] *2010* through June 30, [2010] *2011*; (C) $82,620,000 for migrant and seasonal farmworker programs under section 167 of the WIA, including $76,710,000 for formula grants (of which not less that 70 percent shall be for employment and training services), $5,400,000 for migrant and seasonal housing (of which not less than 70 percent shall be for permanent housing), and $510,000 for other discretionary purposes, which shall be available for the period July 1, [2009] *2010* through June 30, [2010] *2011*:

Carol D. Mitchell

Chapter 5

Sample Company Time-Card

After reviewing the data above, it is consequential for you to keep track of all hours worked, regular and overtime. Audit and store all of your work check stubs. Double check regular time, training time for a new job, overtime and determine if double-time is recorded correctly on **_EACH_** time card record. Make sure your deductions are correct. Add and subtract your totals to make sure you are being paid accurately for all time worked. Review the sample check stub below. Practice your math, until you are confident that you understand your check stub. Under California Labor Code §§ 226-226.6; Industrial Relations your check should contain the following information:

- Gross wages earned
- Total amount of hours worked
- All Deductions
- Net wages earned
- Date you were paid for including: month, day and year
- Social Security number
- Name and Address of the employer
- Number of piece rates units earned
- Hourly rate of pay

Your Rights

Employment Guide

NEW STARTS SOFTWARE COMPANY				Check No.	48998
1111 W. IMPERIAL HIGHWAY				Check Date:	05/16/2009
SUITE # 111				Period Ending:	05/30/2009
BREA, CA 92821				Pay Frequency:	BI-Weekly
SAMPLE CHECK STUB ONLY					
Doe, Jane E.	ID Number: 50104	Status	Exempt	Tax	State and Local Codes
715 Greater Street - Apartment #16	Base Rate: 30.00	Fed: Single ST1: S ST2:	02 02	Adjustments Fed: State DI/UC: Local	PRI: CA LOC1: LOC3: SEC: LOC2: LOC4:
San Francisco, CA 94110	SSN: 566-00-xxxx				LOC5:

IMPORTANT MESSAGE

HOURS AND EARNINGS		TAXES AND DEDUCTIONS		SPECIAL INFORMATION	
CURRENT AMOUNT		**DESCRIPTION**		**CURRENT**	
DESCRIPTION	HOURS/UNIT	EARNINGS	SOCIAL SECURITY	29.88	
REGULAR	26.0	286.00	MEDICARE	6.99	
TRAINING	16.0	108.00			
OVERTIME	4.0	66.00	SDI/UC	4.34	
DOUBLETIME	1.0	22.00			
			TOTAL	41.21	
	47.0				
			AFTER-TAX DEDUCTIONs		
TOTAL H/E		482.00			

PRE-TAX ITEMS							
TOTAL	482						
	EARNINGS	PRETAX	FIT TAXABLE	LESS TAXES	LESS DEDS	EQ NET PAY	
CURRENT	482.00	0.00	482.00	41.21	0.00	440.79	

Carol D. Mitchell

MORE IMPORTANT PAYROLL TIPS

Never call payroll acting unprofessional because you were shorted money on your paycheck. Humans are not perfect. Moreover, we are all inclined to make errors sometimes. Never use profanity. It is not cool. A mad or pissed-off payroll clerk can find ways to delay you not getting your money. Be smart, at the same time, be serious, and be professional.

1. Find out who the payroll clerk is. Next, e-mail her a precise, (short) message regarding money you were not paid.
2. Copy your check stub, and offer to show it to her for review.
3. Copy your sign-in sheet for the payroll clerk. Be nice.

Your Rights Employment Guide

Chapter 6
Prevent Losing Your Job

Know the smoke before the fire and do all that it takes to keep your job!

Insubordination	Lying on the application	Excessive lateness/absence
Low productivity	Incompetence	Negligence
Sleeping on the job	Violation of safety rules	Harassment
Conviction of crime	Continual ineptitude	Gambling
Stealing	Fighting	Use of alcohol/drugs

Tell somebody. To stay on top of your job avoid putting yourself in the line of fire. If you find that your regular work hours are not going to work for you, ask the Company for flex time. Explain to them briefly verbally, and in writing why you need to change your hours. And then, if you are going to be late, call your supervisor, then copy the message to your voice mail to prove that you made the call regarding your lateness. Never take it upon yourself to just come to work late without telling someone.

Be honest. Tell the truth on your application. If this is the right job for you, and everything is going well, if you lied on your application it will without fail come back to bite you when you least expect it. If you do not do anything else in this guide, do not lie on your application. Well-documented cases of employees who have lied on their application reveals that many flourished for years in their positions until they were found out. Regardless of all the fortuitous years these employees gave to the Company, once the lie was revealed, they were fired.

Carol D. Mitchell

AVOID THE PAPER TRAIL

The Paper Trail is their secret weapon and keeping track of you can be their savanna. Fear not, because the paper trail can work for you as well. They maintain the practices of keeping track of you to build an unassailable defense against you in court and to establish a cause and effect equation that you engaged in prohibited behavior causing them to fire you. Keep that in mind, when you use your personalized hand-sheet to give you a winning advantage on your job. Do your job. Never give your employer a reason to hound your every move.

YOUR ACCESS TO PERSONNEL RECORDS

Your personnel records are the property of the employer. Check state law because federal law does not require the employer to give employees access to their personnel file. If you are a federal employee and have an issue regarding your rights and obligations of union, management and employees in a federal workplace represented by a labor union, contact the **Federal Labor Relations Authority** (FLRA) at http://www.flra.gov/. For other employees, all files should only contain job-related information, documentation. At least twenty states including California, Illinois and Massachusetts do let employees into their files. Ask to see the contents of your personnel file regularly in writing, at least twice a year. Be prepared to make copies of this file and literally defend anything in that file that is unfamiliar and outlandish to you.

New Stuff:

Resource: http://www.dol.gov/esa/ofccp/TAguides/sbguide.htm#Q10

Federal contractors are required to maintain any personnel or employment records made or kept by the contractor.

Examples of records that must be maintained:

- Job descriptions
- Job postings and advertisements
- Records of job offers
- Applications and resumes
- Interview notes
- Tests and test results

Your Rights
Employment Guide

- Written employment policies and procedures
- Personnel files

Inside tip: Employers may not want you to have your file if the information in the file will be used to support a legal claim against the Company. Keep your own records to match whatever grievances or conflict your employer may try to boast against you. Ask for copies of everything. If your name is on it, get a copy. Preserve it. If the information contained on work documents is not true or correct, dispute it immediately, *(in writing)*. **<u>Remember:</u>** when you are in a fight against your employer, generally, the burden of proof lies with the employer. If your personal work records are as meticulous and straight as theirs are, you have an increased chance of winning your rightful claim against the employer. When the employer discovers that you know your rights, chances are they will not ride you so hard on the small things. Then, you will have time to go on and be the great employee that you are!

What *they* keep track of
- Your mistakes
- Your conflicts
- Your complaints
- Your work performance

What *you* keep track of
- Your mistakes
- Your conflicts
- Your complaints
- Your work performance
- Specific times dates
- Witnesses (willing or unwilling)

When you get your performance appraisal, look for the comment(s) section. No matter how

Carol D. Mitchell

small the comments box is, write the correct version of your performance appraisal from your own point of view and then ask co-workers to rate your performance and send them to you in an inter-office email. Take the good e-mails home and store them in a safe place. When it is time for you to advance towards a higher position, produce your positive ratings from co-workers and give them to your supervisor as leverage in getting that higher paying position. **Note**: It is okay to add pages to your performance appraisal. Give yourself a chance to better clarify your duties in a manner that your employer was not perhaps aware.

Your Rights

Employment Guide

GET FIRED THE RIGHT WAY

Never *voluntarily quit* your job and lose dollars due to you under unemployment insurance. If you simply do not want to be fired, *(and you have another job lined up,)* then quitting would be a practicable option. In any case, if you are going to stick it out make sure the following things are in play before your employment with your job is terminated.

1. Make sure your employer has given you a fair chance to improve and prove to you in writing that you knew your job was at risk before the termination ensued.
2. Make sure the employer did not breach your employment contract.
3. Make sure the employer did not act intentionally to breach your contract.
4. Make sure the employer follows all federal laws regarding your final paycheck. It is California law to give you the final check <u>immediately</u> upon dismissal. *(This rule may not apply to other states.)*
5. Ask for severance pay and or all benefits due to you including stock options.

6. Ask for a *positive* letter of recommendation from the Department of Human Resources, even if you do not think that you deserve it. In a mutual separation from a job, you have more bargaining power than you realize. **Reminder**: during the separation process preserve your dignity be cool, never fight, act crazy or threaten employees or employment staff, or anyone that let you go. Think ahead! Put forth confidence in your closing actions; present a professional demeanor, and then prepare to just move right on to a better job! Apply for unemployment insurance the next working day that you are let go regardless if you are fired. If you lose unemployment benefits, you may win back wages in the California Unemployment Insurance appeals process.

Carol D. Mitchell

Chapter 7
Labor Law

FYI - Labor Interest/New Law

Few people know that *The California Unemployment Board of Appeals*, *The Department of Labor,* and other state/government entities are waiting to help you, *(the cheated employee)*. New laws are always being implemented towards preserving your being treated fair on the job. <u>New Law: 2004</u> sharing *penalties **SB 1809** has changed the sharing of any penalty that is recovered as a result of an employee lawsuit. Previously any penalty was split 50% to the General Fund, 25% to the Agency and 25% to the employee. Now 75% goes to the Agency specifically designated for enforcement and education of employers and employees of their rights and obligations under the Labor Code. The remaining 25% still go to the employee along with attorney's fees.*

State workers can be overworked and underpaid and in many offices, they do not have the special updated equipment or amenities that are abundant in private industry. When you go to state agencies to get forms always be nice to them and know what forms you need. What's New!

Getting Legal Help

In the past six years, complaints by employees regarding unpaid overtime have nearly doubled - a number that doesn't include suits filed under state law. It is interesting to note that these unpaid overtime complaints have not been limited to service employees such as wait staff or retail workers. Rather, they also include employees who earn higher wages, such as stockbrokers.

Under the Fair Labor Standards Act (FLSA), U.S. employees are allowed a number of protections, including premium pay - or overtime - for hours worked in excess of the 40-hour maximum. The overtime premium rate is 150% of normal pay, commonly known as "time-and-a-half". Unfortunately, many hard-working employees who are entitled to overtime are

Your Rights
Employment Guide

being denied compensation by their employers. Unpaid overtime disputes have grown sharply in recent years, with more and more American workers alleging violations of the FLSA and related state laws.

If you have been denied your fairly earned overtime wages, fill out the form below or call 1-800-654-1475. You may be entitled to compensation.

You have to bring your hand-sheet or diary, your charts, and your witnesses, most important of all, you must always come with the truth, *and nothing but the truth* so help you God.

FYI - Smart tip:

If you ever watch *Judge Joe Brown* or *Judge Judy* on television, they will tell you to "chill out" when you are ahead. The same goes for other legal venues.

When you are winning, "don't say a word." Be **quiet** and listen to the judge telling your company off for forty minutes and you will automatically grow a new skin from all of the pain your employer put you through. Sit back at the governing table in your state issued gummy brown wrought iron chair. Draw a deep breath, relax and enjoy the idea that your super power employer has shortly, lost control. Luxuriate in the fact that the company you had battled with for a year over a measly $550.00 in overtime payments, is about to pay you. Finally, pat yourself on the back for riding *your green rights* wagon up to the Board of Directors and then to the Department of Labor. Congratulations! Finally, you are about to win!

Big brother wants employers to get their *ACT* together

When *The Department of Labor Board* uncovers illegal pay practices in companies, they do not like it. The *National Labor Relations Board,* (NLRB) is designed to conduct investigations and hold hearings involving allegations of unfair labor practices. The NLRB holds and conducts union representation elections, and these elections may involve the certification or de-certification of a union as a bargaining representative of a group of employees and all of this is and was done to preserve your rights.

Employers cannot interfere with unionization; management cannot threaten employees, who engage in organizational activities; or take steps designed to erode employees' support for a

Carol D. Mitchell

union and management cannot make persuasive statements during the pre-election discussion of a union's merits.

The Department of Labor has a lot of power, and by the time, you need them, they will be fair. The next time someone tells you to get your act together, consider four (4) very important facts you can shoot back at them:

Norris-LaGuardia Act: This act, which was passed in 1932, restricts federal courts from issuing injunctions to prevent legal union activities. State courts are not restricted in a similar manner.

Wagner Act: Passed in 1935, this law is formally known as the National Labor Relations Act. This act formally recognized the employee's right to organize and participate in union activities. The Wagner Act created the National Labor Relations Board and established five unfair labor practices by management.

Taft-Hartley Act: This amendment to the Wagner Act was adopted in 1947. It was designed to adjust the bargaining process, which Congress perceived as favoring the unions. Among its important provisions, the *Taft-Hartley Act* provided an 80-day cooling-off period, outlawed the closed shop contract, allowed employers to have free speech, and created the Federal Mediation and Conciliation Service. As a step to balancing the bargaining process, this act also included unfair labor practices by unions.

Landrum-Griffin Act: This also is an amendment to the Wagner Act. It was passed in 1959. The major purpose of this act is to remove corruption from the internal government of unions and to ensure each union's members a specific bill of rights.

Never allow the intimidation factor by anyone to stop you from pursuing your employment rights. Where self-doubt and ambiguity lingers, consult with an employment attorney for sound legal advice! You may have a fantastic chance to recover losses from a variety of employment issues, and a legal pro will be all too willing to make those claims for you!

Your Rights
Employment Guide

IT'S YOUR RIGHTS

It takes patience to fight hard, but you need to know that if you wait for what is due to you, you go to bed feeling happy when you win and you know you are right. Do not second-guess your feelings. If you are going to be leaving a job that hurt you, do not give up. File your paper work with *Small Claims* court, or *The Department of Fair Employment & Housing*, or *The Department of Labor*. It will be a few weeks before your hearing. Never give up. Fight with the truth. File all the right papers and wait for your hearing or court date with patience. Lies are bad. Unfortunately, the opposing side will lie sometimes. Just be prepared. Deal with your case honestly, and then if anyone ever tries to take that from you, you fight like hell to defend your good honor.

HOW TO FILE A COMPLAINT

To File a Pre-Complaint Inquiry you may select one of the following methods:

Use the Department's online system.
Call the Communication Center at 800-884-1684 (voice). If you are deaf or hard of hearing, please call 800-884-1684 (voice) or 800-700-2320 (TTY) or email contact.center@dfeh.ca.gov
Use the Pre-Complaint Inquiry form that matches your issue, complete and return it via U.S. mail to any of DFEH's office locations (http://www.dfeh.ca.gov/Offices.htm).
E-mail the Pre-Complaint Inquiry form to contact.center@dfeh.ca.gov.
If you have a disability that prevents you from submitting a written pre-complaint form on-line, by mail, or email, the DFEH can assist you by scribing your pre-complaint by phone or for individuals who communicate by American Sign Language through the relay system. Contact the Communication Center 800-884-1684 (voice) or 800-700-2320 (TTY) or by email to contact.center@dfeh.ca.gov to schedule an appointment.
The DFEH **will continue** to accept online complaint filings for persons who do not wish for the DFEH to investigate their complaint. Instead, request an immediate Right to Sue.
Then, even if you lose, you win. You only lose when you ***do not exercise your rights at all***.

Carol D. Mitchell

Many laws have been put into play for your protection and the governing professionals know when somebody is lying. You need to wear armor of protection and zealously defend your interest. You need to know how to deal with pressure and not let it stop you from defending and getting what is rightfully yours. **Remember:** Rome really was not built in one day, and neither will be your victory!

Your Rights

Employment Guide

Use it or we lose it!

Special agencies put a lot of work into protecting your employment rights. If you do not use these rights, we may lose them. That would be sad for the little people, like you and me and the regular every day worker.

With that in mind, I will address the secrets that you did not know about government agencies.

- State and government agencies can be your best friend
- State and government agencies have little patience for the ***lazy employer***
- Be prepared. The <u>government and state agencies</u> can be your champion.

NOTE: People that work for the state and the government know the essential value of the word holiday. Generally, private industry workers enjoy fewer holidays than state or government workers do and, they do not care about "all" holidays as do the state, and government agencies.

Carol D. Mitchell

Make sure your job complies with employment law

From day one on a new job, look for the colorful, *"Required Posters for the Workplace."* Search for the posters in the kitchen or the copy room, and familiarize yourself with the Occupational Safety and Health Administration (OSHA) laws, workers compensation, Equal Employment Opportunity Commission, EEOC and the Department of Fair Employment and Housing, DFEH[2] laws. *(See posters ahead).* Learn who the company doctor is on the OSHA posters in case you get hurt on the job and look for the treatment facilities address and telephone number.

Note: Research and apply all new material, provisions to current year's law

The newly reformed law went into effect August 12, 2004. Two provisions apply retroactively to January 1, 2004: Lawsuits for most violations of posting, notice, agency reporting or filing requirements are now excluded from the onerous penalties and private enforcement, except those relating to mandatory payroll or workplace injury reporting; and a court must review and approve penalties in connection with any settlement agreement. *FYI: (Remember to always check for current updates on law related subjects.)*

Remember: You have the right to complain to the Occupational Safety and Health Administration, OSHA about safety and health concerns without being penalized for doing so by your employer.

The employee may file a lawsuit if:

> Violations of Labor Code Division 5, which regulates occupational health and safety, except sections 6310, 6311 and 6399.7 requires that before filing a lawsuit, an employee must notify the employer and the Division of Occupational Safety and Health (DOSH), and copy the Agency.
>
> If your work place is unsafe, in some situations you have the right to refuse to work. To learn more about California OSHA laws call CAL/OSHA Consultation Services in Sacramento, CA at:**1-800-963-9424 or 916-263-0704**

Sample Personal Evaluation

---

[2] DFEH is the Department of Fair Employment and Housing, a California Fair Employment Practices Agency or FEPA. Most states have such agencies whose functions are to enforce federal as well as state anti-discrimination statutes and other provisions of state or federal law.

Your Rights

Employment Guide

EMPLOYEE EVALUATION

Employee Name: Jane A. Doe   **Date:** January 8, 2_____

Employee Position: Office Manager   **Date:** Last review: 01/08/2_____

Supervisor's Name: Betsy XYZ   **Title:** Human Resources Manager - West

Employee Signature:

Directions: *Please complete this evaluation and forward it to your manager one week before your review.*

Achievement of Objectives

Rate the employee on a scale of 1 – 5 for each of the following skill areas:

1 – Insufficient, clear development needs
2 – Needs improvement
3 – Good, successful performance
4 – Excellent performance
5 – Exceptional performance

Carol D. Mitchell

		Rating	Comments (Sample Answers)
Core Skills	Communication	4	I communicate well with everybody in the office including vendors.
	Team Skills	5	I am a team player. I am always assisting others when I can.
	Leadership	4	I am fluid in this role. I have successfully been able to problem solve as well as integrate innovative ideas into my position.
	Financial Management	4	I am open to learning more; and, my great budgeting skills have kept us in the black.
	Organizational Building	5	I am great when it comes to creating organization from scratch. I have done so here and I am always open to learning new things.
	Overall Core Skills	4	Objectively, I am still in the learning process and am willing to grow professionally. My core skills are: communication and organization.

Responsibilities: *List your (sample) major responsibilities of your current position.*

GOALS AND OBJECTIVES:

Please list your goals and objectives for the next review period. (I.e. additional responsibilities, skills to acquire, training to complete, improvement areas to focus on etc.)

General Comments:

Your Rights
Employment Guide

Get to know yourself well enough to present your core skills and abilities. Add sheets to explain your position more fully!

You are not a bad person. You show up for work on time and you do your job. Say you are in your tenth month, and your supervisor has yet to tell you anything negative or positive about how you are doing on your job. You should be worried! You used your hand-sheet from this guide to evaluate your employment and project input. You even worked overtime. So, why then are you about to be let go by your employer? Study these important clues and prepare yourself to get answers from your manager or supervisor when RED FLAGS go up!

1. The boss has time for Nelly but no time for you. (Red Flag)
2. You have no work, paper planes are piling up. (Red Flag)
3. Nelly is doing your job; right in front of you. (Red Flag)
4. Negative feedback, from everyone begins. (Red Flag)
5. Red jelly doughnut drippings land on a classified ad of your job. (Red Flag)

Tipsy time: No. Do not get a drink, but think. Talk it out and get feedback from people at work you trust. Then ask to meet with your supervisor privately. Show her/him your hand-sheet input pointing out project participation and completion of projects that they may not have been aware of. And then, if nothing changes, start wisely looking for another job *__on your own personal time__*. Use this guide to explore and evaluate your many job options. Check out the best and worst job list. Next time choose a career that is more suitable for your talent. Do not quit your job, ever.

Carol D. Mitchell

Chapter 8
Fired

Being fired canned, or let go is no laughing matter. However, the true reality of today's faced paced technological world is that more than a quarter of American workers will be fired at least once in their working career and that does not necessarily mean that it was "all" your fault. It is likely that as you are reading this book someone is being fired. I have done the cooked walk before and I have seen others do it before me.

I maintain like many innocent workers that I never deserved it and the whole getting fired process is nothing short of mortifying and humiliating. Read how Nadine House handled her cook walk. See if you can avoid being the next to do the "Cooked Walk."

How the Cooked Walk begins

I am Nadine House, a 43-year-old mother of 3 and wife of a disabled and unemployed veteran, and today I will be fired. Five O'clock arrived, on a Friday of course. The manager halted, and asked me, *"Can I see you in the Mount Everest Conference Room at five?"* I said, "yes". Mount Everest is the biggest conference room of four in the company. Each room was named after a famous mountain, and the idea for that was mine. I remember the day we mulled over names. I was the captain of the team then. Everyone loved it when my great idea for conference rooms day rendered me to be the company's innovative winner. I won a gold plaque with my name on it that my whole family was proud of. That jubilation lasted about a week. How soon they forget. Now, a few years later, they picked the *Mount Everest Conference* room to fire me in. I had read that companies usually like to fire employees in the boardroom, or someplace that would allow the employee to call somebody a rotten bitch or dirty bastard and I never thought it would ever happen to me. The article I read said that they usually let you say two or three cuss words. Then of course, you have to stop venting and swearing or they, (meaning the employer) will call security.

When the firing committee left, I looked around my cubicle for the last time and I wanted to cry but I did not want my team members at work to see me leaving in tears. I paced myself slowly. *No need to hurry when the consequences of my career had already been decided.* At 4:59 p.m., I marched slowly past two tired gray Cannon fax machines and one dirty white

Your Rights
Employment Guide

water cooler with the light blue spigot for cold water, and the bright red spigot for the hot water side that never worked. I was on my way to face the firing squad. I felt like the dead woman walking when I took the cooked walk. Depression caused my heads up will to shatter. I felt numb as my chin bowed into my chest. News spreads fast. Glaring eyes sat on top the brims of row after row of awful gray cubicles. The curious co-workers were the lucky ones. They were now the gainfully employed and they watched me, the dead woman walking move downward to my destiny. Depression, embarrassment and humiliation afforded me a hazy cloud to block out the onlookers. People began to whisper, *"what happened?"* They knew it was over for me. After five years with the company, sales were low.

The title, *"Retail Manager"* had been on the cutting block for a year. I was surprised this day had not come sooner. Slow sales? What could I do? I wanted to cry, and go to the bathroom, but the walk, that awful walk down that long hallway decorated with picture after picture of successful sales ingénues, took forever. My nerves were shattered. Mount Everest housed the HR manager who was sitting with my supervisor Darlene; both were drinking the last of Hills Brothers burnt coffee offerings.

The HR person smoothed her pale white hands over a fat Manila paper trail file. "Go ahead and sit in the gray chair Nadine," Darlene said. I sat. Next, my supervisor got up and closed the conference room door. When she returned to her seat, she offered me some burnt coffee. I said no, intentionally leaving off the "thank you". I eased into the hard gray chair and held back my tears as the sudden strong urge to release myself lifted my butt out of the chair. I bit my lip. Then I straightened my back to hear their excuses on why I was about to be fired.

I became humble as I listened to the manager tell the HR person that I was dumb and could not catch on to the new sales approach in the company.

Her statements belied the three years I had been honored as the employee of the year. She said that my inability to catch on quickly and be a team player was the reason that they were letting me go. I had wanted to learn the new procedures faster. I worked overtime to learn pages and pages of retail new-age objectives. Unfortunately, I had not received the proper training for the new sales objectives. Therefore, I failed by their estimation and before long

Carol D. Mitchell

there was talk in the industry that they were replacing me with a twenty-year old. Nevertheless, I accepted my fate and held back my tears. I was offered and I rejected the severance package because I was going to fight for my rights. I had my own paper trail and eyewitnesses to prove my case, and I had three employee of the year awards. The company I loved discarded me, and I knew it was going to be hard for me to find another job over forty.

After the firing, I hired a big firm employment law attorney to file claims for overtime and age discrimination, intentional infliction of emotional distress and defamation of character. My great work record forced the employer to defend letting me go. Their policy was inconsistent. Their contract with me was clearly implied and their mission statement all but promised me a permanent job if I stayed in my job over two years. Two years later at the trial the employer came prepared with documentation. However, I knew my rights and what they had was insufficient according to the jury. I had documented better than they had.

My performance evaluations were excellent. Furthermore, I had the chance to show the jury my awards. I was able to present cogent evaluation "comments" input, times, dates and witnesses to corroborate my side of the firing. Seven out of twelve jurors cried openly in court for me. The judge hated the employer's excuse for letting me go. However, most important of all, I had employment laws on my side. I was not nasty to my former employer. I was however, prepared. Armed with facts and the truth, in the end I won three times my former salary. In this case, the lawyer settled to keep the employer from filing a drawn out appeal. I was happy that I had kept all my smart notes on my snappy *"My rights," hand-sheet*. From the moment my employer stopped listening to my input at work, I wrote everything down. My employer called me dumb, and I wrote that down and helped my case significantly by writing down all dates and times. In essence, I was merely a human being trying to make an honest living for my family and I hung in there and won!

NEWSFLASH! *Judges do not like it when employers fire employees for not catching on or for not knowing how to do the job! Nadine intuitively took advantage of her rights. For three-years she kept important e-mails and she wrote things down. Keeping her files at home, Nadine was a good employee who ended up being a victim of circumstances. The judges, administrative law judges, and employee advocates of the world want to hear that you are at work every day as Nadine was. They want to know that you tried to do your job right and that you were dependable as Nadine was. They want to see that you did not voluntarily quit your*

Your Rights
Employment Guide

job or threaten your supervisor, and if you tangibly prove to the judge all of that and show them all your accumulated great note keeping facts, chances are you will win your case just as Nadine won her case. Your employer will lose against you with a reprimand from the court. Win or lose, you can then take pride that you did the right thing for you.

Remember: If you need an employment lawyer, NELA is the country's only professional organization that is exclusively comprised of lawyers who represent individual employees in cases involving employment discrimination and other employment-related matters. The headquarters is located in San Francisco, California.

Consult the yellow pages of your telephone book, or go look for one on the computer[3]. I am not a lawyer, but I can help you with the basic fundamental tools to help yourself that I have acquired in my long work history. For

more fun secrets read on, and make sure to run wallet size copies of sample letters and charts and other fun things from this guide to carry with you at all times.

More tips:

You have the right to sue an employer for **"wrongful disciplinary actions,"** even if you do not get fired! It's 2009. We are facing the most difficult job market and employment situation ever. Protecting your interest will make the difference between keeping or losing your job. Nobody will be able to defend your interest better than you will.

Example: One day Susan X was humiliated by her boss when he called her a fat pig and then he directed outrageous, offensive slurs at her. After this humiliating circumstance, Susan asked the Department of Human Resources to move her to another work area. When Susan X was granted her move she attempted to go back to her old cubicle to pack her things. Next, her old boss refused to let her get her personal property, and then he told her he knew she was not coming back, so he threw all of her family pictures away.

---

[3] Again an excellent source for finding an employment law attorney is the National Employment Lawyers Association (NELA) at www.nela.org

Carol D. Mitchell

Susan X did all the right things. She reported her boss immediately to the right personnel. Then, she stayed calm and professional. After a complete investigation of the aforementioned matter, Susan kept her job and won $75,000.00 in damages for her old bosses "wrongful disciplinary" actions, humiliation, defamation of character, and for possibly a few other things as well. Remember to always be cool.

1. Tell the offender to cease and desist
2. Record such events in your diary
3. Report it immediately to the Department of Human Resources
4. Get names, dates and correct times of all witnesses to such an event

KNOW WHAT CLAIM TO FILE

☐ A regular California claim if you worked in California in a job covered by the unemployment insurance law even if you now reside outside California.

☐ A federal claim if your employment was in civilian work for the federal government or as a member of the Armed Forces (*benefit costs are paid from federal funds*).

☐ An interstate claim if earnings were in another state. If you worked in another state in the last 24 months, you may be able to file a claim. This includes the District of Columbia, Canada, Puerto Rico, and the Virgin Islands.

☐ A combined wage claim if you have earnings in more than one state in specified times. This type of claim could increase your Unemployment Insurance benefits. For base periods and more, call one of the numbers below.

Unemployment Insurance Call Information:

English: 1-800-300-5616   Vietnamese: 1-800-547-2058
Spanish: 1-800-326-8937   TTY (Non Voice)   1-800-815-9387
Cantonese 1-800-547-3506
How to file a claim
Resource: http://www.edd.ca.gov/unemployment/filing_a_claim.htm
Filing a State of California Unemployment Insurance Claim
Claim Process
This section provides a step-by-step summary of the UI claim process.

Your Rights
Employment Guide

1. Employers give a copy of the booklet, <u>For Your Benefit - California's Programs for the Unemployed, DE 2320</u> to employees who are unemployed. The <u>UI Code, Section 1089</u> requires employers to provide the booklet.
2. The individual files a claim for UI benefits using one of the following methods:
   - Access <u>eApply4UI</u>:
     The eApply4UI application is available on the Main menu of this Web site. Answers to questions are entered online. After the application is completed the individual submits it online to the Department. **Note:** This is the fastest way to file your claim.
   - <u>Contact EDD</u> by telephone.
     Individuals will speak to a Department representative who will ask a series of questions and record the responses.
   - Complete a <u>UI Application, DE 1101I</u>:
     This form is available in the <u>Forms and Publications</u> section of this Web site. The DE 1101I is printed, completed by hand and either faxed or mailed to the Department.

   Note: The above options may also be used to reactivate an existing claim or file for extended benefits.
3. The Department representative files the claim and the following documents are mailed:

   To Claimants
   - A Guide to Benefits and Employment Services, DE 1275A
   - Notice of Unemployment Insurance Award, DE 429Z
   - Notice of Unemployment Insurance Claim Filed, DE 1101CLMT
   - CalJOBS^{SM} brochure, DE 2456

Carol D. Mitchell

To Employers

Notice of Unemployment Insurance Claim Filed, DE 1101CZ

4. The EDD decides if a claimant is eligible to collect benefits. To make this decision, we conduct telephone interviews with claimants, employers or their representatives and review statements submitted in writing.
5. After we make a decision, we mail a Notice of Determination or Notice of Determination/Ruling, DE 1080CT to claimants who do not qualify for benefits. We also mail a DE 1080CT to employers who respond in writing and within time limits about a quit, discharge, or other issues that may prevent payment of benefits.
6. Employers or claimants who disagree with our written decision have the right to appeal the decision.
7. Claimants complete and submit a form for each week they wish to claim benefits. The forms are usually for two weeks at a time and claimants must certify that they have met eligibility requirements for each week benefits are claimed.
8. After the Department pays the claimant the first week of benefits, we mail a Notice of Wages Used for Unemployment Insurance Claim, DE 1545 to the claimant's base period employer(s). Base period employers may be charged for all or part of a claimant's benefits.
9. To ensure accuracy, base period employer(s) review the information reported on the DE 1545. The form shows the claimant's identity, wage and employment information. The base period employer(s) use the DE 1545 to notify the Department about separation information and to correct errors on wages reported to EDD. The time limits for reporting separation information is 15 days from the date the form was mailed. Wage corrections must be reported within 20 calendar days from the date the DE 1545 was mailed.

Your Rights

Employment Guide

10. A Department representative reviews a base period employer's response to the DE 1545 and decides if the employer's account will be charged for the claimant's benefits. The EDD mails a Notice of Ruling, DE 1080CT to the employer who submitted separation information within the time limits. A favorable or unfavorable decision that is sent to a base period employer(s) does not usually change a claimant's entitlement to benefits.

11. A base period employer who disagrees with EDD's written decision may file an appeal.

WHY? Your employer pays into this insurance to provide you with an income when you are out of work through no fault of your own.

Carol D. Mitchell

Internet Services:

www.edd.ca.gov

Recording more of your time

All the time that you put into resolving a workplace problem are considered "hours worked." Therefore, the employer is required to pay you regular rates and regular overtime for over 8 hours. Code Sections 200,1174 1195.5; Industrial Welfare Commission Orders 1-3, 6-10, 13, 14 Title 29 U.S. Code Sections 201-219 785.42.

Your Rights Employment Guide

Chapter 9
The Resources Manager

Question: The most important person you should know at work:
Jeopardy Answer: Who is the Human Resources Manager

The Human Resources Manager does a lot more than file department records and conduct new employee orientations. This is the most important resource you should know in the company. Therefore, it will not hurt you to learn who this person is and make them your strongest work alliance.

The Human Resources person develops and administers HR plans and procedures for all personnel. This person organizes and controls essentially all activities of the department and participates in developing departmental goals, objectives and systems with assistance to the corporate executives in the company. Employment laws guide this person strictly. In common words: The Human Resources Manager has a powerful influence in the company and she or she maintain imminent power in settling employment and money issues with you more swiftly really than anyone else in the company. Presidents, and Company vice presidents, do not want to deal with run of the mill problems that can be resolved below their level. A good HR person has excellent bargaining knowledge, and superb resolution skills.

The Human Resources Manager, updates compensation programs, and rewrites job descriptions as necessary; conducts annual salary surveys and develops merit pool (salary budgets). This person is the most prominent guide you have to get your point across to middle and upper management. *Find out whom the HR person is and if you want to take them to Starbucks one day, that would be a great strategic move on your part.* Seriously, she/he controls personnel policies, procedures and they regularly update the employee handbook manuals and it will never hurt for the HR person to know first-hand what a great employee you are.

Carol D. Mitchell

Smart share tip:

When the judge saw how behind in times Rick's former job was with payroll record keeping, she tore into the company over everything from having illegal pay stubs to why the hell they had him working for straight time on Thanksgiving Day. The judge said: "You paid Rick Davis under time here. Then, you paid him over time there. Which time is the right time for Rick Davis?" The HR person had never been a real professional and in the judge's estimation, she did not like Rick Davis. Just like the company in question, she never took Rick's employment wage rights seriously. Wearing a white, fishing cap, and an orange windbreaker, with a pair of faded, blue Levi's her attire in itself was an insult to the judge. To make matters worse, this HR person was visibly shaken. After she lifted off her cap, her attempts to tame her wild blond curls was a lost cause. She told the judge that payroll was not her job. Rick wanted to laugh, but Rick read this guide and he showed up in front of the judge prepared. Rick had seen a few episodes of Judge Judy and Judge Mathis and he knew how to behave in a court of law. Rick spoke only when he was asked to by the judge and he addressed all of his answers to the magistrate with "yes sir/ma'am" or "no sir/ma'am" and he made no comments to his employer. The grilling of the human resources person by the judge began to feel better than a cold bath on a hot day to Rick Davis! He had been denied his overtime for over two years and as much as he enjoyed it, memories of his long fight to fairness quieted his need for expression. Preparedness, professionalism and great note taking rendered a sound judgment in favor of Rick Davis in the full amount of $36,000.00.

Your Rights
Employment Guide

Required Work Posters
& More
Required Posters

The following is a chart of current required posters for California employers. You have the most current posters if you have a *California Chamber of Commerce Employer Poster with "2009" in the upper right corner*. Remember: **Note: Apply all new material to your current year's law**

The chart is arranged in the order the posters appear on the Chamber's Employer Poster, available at http://www.calchamberstore.com.

Required posters must be displayed at each work site and must be in an area accessible to all employees. Generally speaking, the most current version of each poster must be displayed. State and federal agencies periodically make changes to required posters. To find out about poster updates after the date of this printing go to http://www.hrcalifornia.com/poster.

Log 300 - Not every employer must comply with Cal/OSHA's Log 300 record keeping requirements.

- Find out whether your company is required to record workplace injuries and illnesses using the Exempt Wizard at http://www.hrcalifornia.com/log300
- Download the Log 300 forms from *http://www.hrcalifornia.com/log300*

Other - Unique posters and notices may be required depending on certain circumstances such as heavy equipment or forklifts, chemical use, and government contracts.

*Both the state and federal minimum wage posters must be posted, even though California's minimum wage is currently higher than the federal minimum wage.

Carol D. Mitchell

Your smart samples of "exempt" and "non-exempt" employees

TYPICAL EXEMPT JOBS	TYPICAL NON-EXEMPT JOBS
• Department Head	• Data Entry Clerk
• Financial Consultant	• Front Desk Receptionist
• Doctor or Physician	• Customer Service Clerk
• Credit Manager	• Secretary
• Account Executive	• Bank Teller
• Personal Director	• Newspaper Reporter
• Lawyer (Attorney)	• Bookkeeper
• Tax Specialist	• Trainee

Your Rights
Employment Guide

READERS NOTES:

IWC Wage Orders - All employers must post the industry-specific Wage Order appropriate to their business, with a "Summary" in front of it. Visit http://www.hrcalifornia.com/wageorderwizard for help with selecting the correct wage order for your business.

EMPLOYEE SMART TIPS

1. Employees working 20 hours or more a week are usually eligible for holiday pay.
2. Holiday pay is your regular straight time rate for the number of hours in an 8-hour workday.
3. An employee typically has to work the day before the holiday and the day after the holiday to get paid for the holiday.
4. When the holiday crashes on a Saturday, the preceding Friday is then usually considered the Company holiday. When the holiday falls on Sunday, then the next Monday will usually be the Company holiday.
5. Out of paid status, employees are not eligible for holiday pay. So, wait until you are off your disability or layoff to get holiday pay benefits.
6. Regular employees who work on a holiday will get one and one half times their regular pay rate. Biweekly employees who work a holiday that falls on their regular day off will be paid at twice their regular rate and receive another day off with pay. (*Talk to your HR person for more details about holiday pay. Different companies may have varying policies regarding holidays and pay.*)

STANDARD HOLIDAY POLICY

Some players go right into a job and the first thing they want to know is: "When is the next holiday. Be smart and recognize that everybody ain't celebrating Martin Luther King Holiday, (especially) in private industry. So, if it is your partner's birthday, or your mama's birthday, chances are it is not a holiday for the Company!

7. Make sure that payroll knows holiday pay is not to be considered hours worked in the figuring of overtime.

Carol D. Mitchell

REMINDERS

Employee coverage via union or negotiated contracts will follow holiday pay as is laid out in specific bargaining terms. If you are an active member of a union, meet with your Shop Steward, or delegate to acquire a full picture of your union contract rights.

CLAIM IT –IT'S YOURS

Unfortunately, many workers have had to build up the gall to fight and to that end, many survivors have won big time exercising their special employment rights. You need to know that winning is possible and you need to know that you can get what is rightfully yours. As much as we would like to enjoy the honor system and trust our employer, times have changed and the need for continual evidence forces us to write things down. Know your rights, claim it, it's yours and you have the power to get it. An employee without rights is like a phantom without his mask. Be ready for the employer and the employer will be ready to treat you with the fairness and respect that you deserve on the job.

MAINTAIN GOOD RECORD KEEPING

At the beginning and in the middle of this guide, you will see the personal time keeping record I have created for you where you can record all of your work time regular and overtime. Copy this form and use it daily to record your time and work events and the hours you spent resolving work related issues. **Reminder**: remember to write special notes for yourself and keep records because tangible facts is a great way to get promoted on the job, or government agencies give special credence to your great calendar and note taking. Having great records is almost a certain way to get you the win you are seeking to prove overtime hours that you may not have gotten paid for.

ALERT AT WORK

I want to be your guiding eyes. I want to assist you in keeping track of your job, to monitor your wages and make sure that not a dime of your overtime payment sits in your employer's bank account earning interest (*for them*) or the rich one(s) on the golf courses across America. Recently, a dear friend of mine had a hearing with the Department of Labor. My friend was

Your Rights

Employment Guide

prepared to fight for her overtime wages, and here is what she found out!

Reminder: It is required under federal law that the employer pay a "non-exempt worker at least one and one half times their regular rates of pay for all hours worked in excess of 40 hours per week. In California, non-exempt employees who work in excess of 8 hours per day earn time and one half for all time worked after 8 hours in one given day and this time is doubled for holiday work.

Carol D. Mitchell

Chapter 10
Your Protected Rights

Preparation is key:
If you ever go to battle with the employer, there are some very important facts that you will need to know:

YOUR FEW PROTECTED RIGHTS

| The Pregnancy Discrimination Act | Title V11 of the Civil Rights Act of 1964 | Equal Pay Act 1963 |
| Age Discrimination in Employment Act 1967 | Americans with Disability Act (ADA) | |

1. Know what the employee handbook says - (*never throw this book away*). Understand the general company policy, statement of goals, working hours. Understand the policy for non-disclosure, procedural policy, pay periods and performance evaluations. Find out what the safety rules are and follow them to the tee. Have respect for company property and telephones. Never make personal calls without permission from your supervisor. At work turn your cell phone off!

2. Know who the management decision makers in the company are - (get a copy of the companies organization chart from their Intranet site and take it home and store it before things go bad.) You need to know where your bargaining power lies, and who the ***powerful, decision making professionals are***, including the HR person, vice president, president, CEO, CIO and all company lenders/shareholders. If you are in a union, ask the shop steward to explain foreign policy to you in terms that you will understand. If you know who puts up front money to keep the company going, it can be an immense bargaining tool for you later.

3. Find out through public records if there are claims against your employer with the Better Business Bureau to use for your advantage, before you submit a demand letter for payment of a claim.

Your Rights

Employment Guide

4. Be aware that (anyone) can write a demand letter to an employer. You don't need an attorney to put someone on notice. Use your Internet savvy to find sample letters on the Internet to help you do things the right way. Key: be prepared.
5. Know who is the Department of Human Resources Manager.
6. Know who the lawyers for the company are and research them.
7. Know the company policy towards your protected classes. If you are over (40), find out about age discrimination policy and procedures.
8. Research issues thoroughly before presenting your case to the employer. *Tip:* the library in your community is a great resource for employment issues and law.

Note: Apply all new material to current year's law

Carol D. Mitchell

SEXUAL HARASSMENT TRUTH/FACTS

Sexual Harassment Defined: Sexual Harassment as defined by the United Stated Equal Employment Opportunity Commission (EEOC): "Unwelcome sexual advances, requests for sexual favors, and other verbal or physical conduct of a sexual nature constitutes sexual harassment when submission to or rejection of this conduct explicitly or implicitly affects an individual's employment, unreasonably interferes with an individual's work performance or creates an intimidating, hostile or offensive work environment." The victim as well as the harasser may be a woman or a man. The victim does not have to be of the opposite sex. The harasser can be the victim's supervisor, an agent of the employer, a supervisor in another area, a co-worker, or a non-employee. The victim does not have to be the person harassed but could be anyone affected by the offensive conduct. Unlawful sexual harassment may occur without economic injury to or discharge of the victim. The harasser's conduct must be unwelcome.

- **Types of Sexual Harassment**: Types of Sexual Harassment There are two legally recognized types of sexual harassment: "Quid Pro Quo" sexual harassment (2) "Hostile Environment" sexual harassment

    Quid Pro Quo: Quid Pro Quo Quid Pro Quo: Quid pro quo sexual harassment occurs when an individual's submission to or rejection of sexual advances or conduct of a sexual nature is used as the basis for employment decisions affecting the individual or the individual's submission to such conduct is made a term or condition of employment. It is sufficient to show a threat of economic loss to prove quid pro quo sexual harassment. A single sexual advance may constitute harassment if it is linked to the granting or denial of employment benefits. Courts have held employers strictly liable for quid pro quo sexual harassment initiated by supervisory employees. A subordinate who submits and then changes her or his mind and refuses can still bring quid pro quo sexual harassment charges.

    Hostile Environment: Hostile Environment Hostile Environment: Hostile

Your Rights
Employment Guide

environment sexual harassment occurs when unwelcome sexual conduct unreasonably interferes with an individual's job performance or creates a hostile, intimidating or offensive work environment even though the harassment may not result in tangible or economic job consequences, that is, the person may not lose pay or a promotion. There are two conditions that determine liability for employers in cases of hostile environment sexual harassment: The employer knew or should have known about the harassment, and The employer failed to take appropriate corrective action

Personal Impact: Personal Impact One study found that fully 50% of women who filed a complaint in California were fired; another 25% resigned due to the stresses of the complaint process or the harassment itself. A study of federal employees reported that those who have been harassed lose $4.4 million in wages and 973,000 hours in unpaid leave each year. 90% to 95% of sexually harassed women suffer from some debilitating stress reaction, including anxiety, depression, headaches, sleep disorders, weight loss or gain, nausea, lowered self-esteem and sexual dysfunction.

Business Impact: Business Impact The costs are borne not only by the victims of harassment; they create financial havoc for employers as well. Sexual harassment costs a typical Fortune 500 company $6.7 million per year in absenteeism, low productivity and employee turnover. That does not include additional costs for litigation expenses, executive time and tarnished public image should a case wind up in court.

Types of Harassment: Types of Harassment California Law defines the following types of harassment Verbal Harassment – Epithets, derogatory comments or slurs Physical Harassment – Assault, impeding or blocking movement, or any physical interference with normal work or movement, when directed at an individual Visual Harassment – Derogatory posters, calendars, cartoons or drawings Sexual Favors – Unwanted sexual advances which condition an employment benefit upon an exchange of sexual favors Gender Harassment – Due to pregnancy, childbirth or related medical conditions

Carol D. Mitchell

Personal Liability: Personal Liability Harassers Are Personally Liable If you, as an employee, are found to have engaged in sexual harassment, or if you as a manager know about the conduct and condone or ratify it, you may be personally liable for monetary damages. Your company does not have to pay for damages assessed against you personally. In addition, the company may take appropriate disciplinary measures, including termination, against any employee who engages in sexual harassment. * Silence + Knowledge = Consent

Federal Law: Federal Law Federal Law, "It's not just a California Thing" Title VII of the Civil Rights Act prohibits harassment of an employee based on race, color, sex, religion, or national origin. The Age Discrimination in Employment Act (ADEA) prohibits harassment of employees who are 40 or older on the basis of age The Americans with Disabilities Act (ADA) prohibits harassment based on disability. All EEOC Statutes prohibit retaliation for complaining of discrimination or participating in complaint proceedings

Federal Law: Federal Law When does Harassment violate Federal Law? Harassment violates federal law if it involves discriminatory treatment based on race, color, sex (with or without sexual conduct), religion, national origin, age, disability, or because the employee opposed job discrimination or participated in an investigation or complaint proceeding under the EEOC statutes. Federal law does not prohibit simple teasing, offhand comments or isolated incidents that are not extremely serious. The conduct must be sufficiently frequent or severe to create a hostile work environment or result in a "tangible employment action," such as hiring, firing, promotion, or demotion.

Discrimination: Discrimination What is Discrimination? Discrimination covers actions taken against people because of their membership, perceived membership, or associated membership in certain protected classes. Discrimination means treating people differently, and disadvantageously, compared with other people not in the same class. Remember that everyone is part of a protected class. Everyone has a race and marital status, is perceived as one gender or another, and associates with people in

Your Rights

Employment Guide

protected classes. Disparate (unequal) treatment Employee or Applicant is treated differently, specifically because of his or her protected class status Disparate (unequal) impact Employment practice that appears neutral on its face but is discriminatory against protected classes in practice (unequal requirements)

Sexual Harassment is against the law. The day you begin your new job read the employee manual and then learn what the Company policy is on harassment and sexual harassment. REMEMBER: It is your right to say no to a person that pursues you on the job. Many companies have stringent policies against sexual harassment. Consult your employee handbook to find out what the policy is and hold the Company accountable to their written policy regarding sexual harassment. Remember to report harassment, and sexual harassment immediately to your supervisor. Tell the harasser to cease and desist. (See the sample cease and desist letter to the offender below.) All employees are entitled to work in an environment that is free of harassment.

Carol D. Mitchell

Chapter 11
Sexual Harassment

AB1825 Sexual Harassment Training

As of 2007, The Fair Employment & Housing Commission (FEHC) has adopted final regulations on AB 1825, the California law that requires employers with more than 50 employees or contractors to provide sexual harassment training to all supervisors. The regulations became effective on August 17, 2007.

Under AB 1825, training for all supervisors **must be repeated every 2 years.** In addition, newly-promoted supervisors and new hires must be trained within 6 months of their promotion and/or hire date.

Employers beware: all training must meet the strict training requirement contained in the final regulations.

Why should I train? What is the penalty for noncompliance?

If one of your employees files a claim of sexual harassment, you can expect **a letter from the Department of Fair Employment & Housing (DFEH) requesting proof that you are in full compliance** with the requirements of AB 1825. The letter will ask that you provide the number of supervisors you employ, the dates training was provided, the name and qualifications of the trainer, and copies of the training material provided. If found to be non-compliant, you can be ordered to train all of your supervisors within 60 days.

Worse yet, your employee's lawyer will argue that failure to train in accordance with the law demonstrates an organization's "reckless disregard" for the law, and thereby establishes a potential basis for punitive damages liability.

The DEFH will demand that you retrain all of your supervisors if they find your previous training does not comply. **We've made it cost-efficient and convenient for you to train everyone in your organization** by offering the course in **three convenient delivery methods**.....so you can pick what works best for you now and avoid costly lawsuits later.

What an AB 1825 Course should Consist of:

Your Rights

Employment Guide

CASE STUDY

How Sally Exercised Her Rights.
During the two-year course of her employment at her former Company Sally, was fondled by the CEO six times. The first time he touched her inappropriately, Sally, asked him to stop and then she reported his conduct to her supervisor. After an in-house investigation disproved Sally's charges, the next time it happened, the CEO told Sally to *"deal with it"* because no one had believed her the first time. He further stated to her that if she wanted to keep her job and get a promotion next year to *"ship up or shape out"*. Then he made sure when he stroked Sally the next five times that nobody was around to see it. Hence, Sally was left with no witnesses to the CEO's detestable behavior. In due course, Sally became ill. Consequently, she started receiving professional counseling for the residual effects of the CEO's persistent harassing behavior. Sally had a stellar work record, and had never been written up or reprimanded by her supervisor before. In fact, her job performance appraisals had all been rated excellent. After the ill-fated investigation, Sally's work output was down. Her work efforts had clearly suffered counter-actively because of the CEO's ongoing actions.

One year after Sally told her supervisor and the Department of Human Resources about the CEO she was fired without cause. Determined to exercise her civil rights under Title VII, Sally contacted each chain of command in her employ to reconcile her claims to no avail. Then Sally wrote a certified letter to Department of Human Resources exemplifying her administrative remedies in accordance with the Company's employment handbook policy.

When all of her administrative opportunities were (fully) expended, within 30 days,

The Department of Fair Employment & Housing, (DFEH) made an appointment to review the facts of Sally's case. On the day of her appointment, Sally presented to them a well-documented case and the Department took her complaint. Later, a copy of the charge was given to Sally. Then, another copy was mailed to her Company.

A week after the charge was filed, Sally found an employment law attorney. Sally, then asked

Carol D. Mitchell

the Department of Fair Employment & Housing, *(in writing)* to dismiss her charge and issue to her a right-to-sue letter against her former Company. Sally now had one year from the date of the issuance of the *right-to-sue* letter to sue her old Company. When the skilled employment law attorney saw how well-prepared Sally was he took her case immediately on contingency leaving Sally free of having to deal with her former Company again.

With attention to detail, <u>*great note taking*</u>, itemizations of correct times and dates, and excellent performance evaluations the attorney acknowledged that Sally had made his job easy by handling her case so well. Great preparation, determination and an excellent work record forced Sally's former employer to settle out of court with her for a total sum of $75,000.00.

> ***NOTE:*** *Before you hire an attorney, check them out through the California Bar Association.*

Retaliation:

Your job can not legally harass you for filing an innocent complaint because it is against the law. Your complaint is in good faith. You participated <u>fully</u> in the Department of Human Resource's investigation, and you told your harasser to cease and desist and you can prove it because you wrote it down in your diary with your other corroborating evidence. If your employer fires you for exercising your rights under a protected class their retaliation against you will be considered a "separate" violation under the Civil Rights Act under title VII of the employment law.

Your Rights

Employment Guide

MORE IMPORTANT NEW LAW

Senate Bill 1809: Curbing the "Sue Your Boss" Law
Senate Bill 1809 took effect immediately and makes several important amendments to the PAGA.

To begin, SB 1809 substantially curbs the PAGA by providing that an aggrieved employee may bring a lawsuit against his or her employer for Labor Code violations only *after* complying with procedural and administrative requirements. Before bringing a lawsuit for most claims, an employee must provide written notice of the alleged claim to his or her employer and to the Labor and Workforce Development Agency. This notice allows the Agency an opportunity to investigate certain specified claims and an employee may bring a lawsuit on these claims only if the Agency chooses not to investigate the claim or does not issue a citation against the employer based on the claim. Moreover, for some claims, an employer will be given an opportunity to avoid a lawsuit by correcting the alleged violation.

Likewise, in regard to claims for violations of health and safety laws, an employee must also provide written notice of the claim to the Division of Occupational Safety and Health (Cal/OSHA) before bringing a lawsuit. The employee may bring a lawsuit on the claim only if Cal/OSHA does not issue a citation to the employer on the claim and the employer fails to correct the alleged violation.

In addition to the procedural requirements for bringing lawsuits under the PAGA, SB 1809 also exempts some of the more minor and technical Labor Code provisions from the Act. Thus, an employee may no longer bring a lawsuit under the PAGA for violations of posting, notice, reporting, or filing requirements of the Labor Code, except where the filing or reporting requirement involves mandatory payroll or workplace injury reporting.

Carol D. Mitchell

Conclusion

Although SB 1809 provides some relief to employers from lawsuits brought under the PAGA, employers must remain cautious and aware of potential claims. Of course, the best way for employers to avoid claims is to take action to ensure that their workplaces are free from Labor Code violations. Certainly, this is no small task considering that the Labor Code is quite dense and contains hundreds of obscure requirements. Nonetheless, taking immediate and comprehensive measures to ensure compliance with the Labor Code is necessary in order for an employer to avoid potential costly and time-consuming lawsuits.

The court could also award attorneys' fees. Not surprisingly, this law resulted in a flurry of anti-employer lawsuits, as hungry attorneys saw an opportunity to cash in on the bill.

Anti-retaliation provisions

In order to protect employees from discrimination or retaliation for giving a notice alleging a violation to the Agency or the employer, or filing a lawsuit, *SB1809* amended Labor Code section 98.6. Protections are included in matters involving:

http://www.leginfo.ca.gov/cgi-bin/calawquery?codesection=lab&codebody=&hits=20
Resource as of May, 2009

- *1195.5.* The Division of Labor Standards Enforcement shall determine, upon request, whether the wages of employees, which exceed the minimum wages fixed by the commission, have been correctly computed and paid. For this purpose, the division may examine the books, reports, contracts, payrolls and other documents of the employer relative to the employment of employees. The division shall enforce the payment of any sums found, upon examination, to be due and unpaid to the employees.

- 1197. The minimum wage for employees fixed by the commission is the minimum wage to be paid to employees, and the payment of a less wage than the minimum so fixed is unlawful.

Your Rights

Employment Guide

SAMPLE CEASE AND DESIST LETTER TO OFFENDER

January 5, 20_____

John Doe, CEO
XXXX
Company XXX
Concord, CA 94520

Mr. John Doe:

On January 02, 20_____ I told you that I was not interested in you. After work on the aforementioned date you pulled up to the bus stop at 5:30 p.m. demanding that I get into the car with you. When I refused, you got out of your car and then you approached me. When I said, I was going to call the police you left. John, this is harassment. I find your actions extremely troublesome and offensive. Therefore, for the second time I am asking you to stop, cease, and desist. If you contact me or stalk me again, I will report you to the police and to your supervisor.

Carol D. Mitchell

DEPARTMENT OF FAIR EMPLOYMENT & HOUSING
YOUR KEYS TO THE MAILBOX AND MORE

(1-800-884-1684)

WWW.DFEH.CA.GOV

State of California

When you have been discriminated against or sexually harassed on your job, you are exhausted! Therefore, you will not have the energy to read all the materials to do things right so that you can win your case. You are reading this guide to implement procedures in the right order to present a cogent case. Don't worry! I am going to break down to you how you must approach the Department of Fair Employment and Housing in a professional manner and in a way that you don't have to stress on. *We will call the following section, Your checklist √*

When the checklist of events as listed below have been reported and exhausted in accordance with the stated procedures of your office manual - you are then ready to file with the DFEH and or the Department of Labor. Many human resource department managers are fair and (do not want you to file cases that will lead to protracted litigation against their Company,) Remember: tell the truth, keep copious notes, dates, places, times and witnesses.

1. √I was discriminated against or harassed

2. √I reported it to my supervisor

3. √I wrote down the events and requested an investigation. I cooperated fully in investigation.

6. √I reported incident to the Department of Human Resources as soon as the events occurred.

7. √I reported the incident to all chains of commands to no avail, and the investigation was closed.

8. √I have exhausted all of my in office remedies in accordance with my companies policies as written in the employee handbook and still I have not been treated fairly, I am being retaliated against.

Your Rights
Employment Guide

4. √I advised the harasser to cease and desist/behavior; I have times, dates, witnesses.

5. √My supervisor has not helped me fully.

9. √I created a binder, on my own time to memorialize all actions in my case. I have given my employer a period to respond to settle my case. I have received no response. I have kept everything in order by dates/times.

10. √My checklist is completed. I will inform the Department of Human Resources in writing that I am going to file a case with the Department of Fair Employment & Housing. If I am ignored, fired, or dismissed, I will proceed forward.

Your checklist is completed, and, now you are ready to proceed on. You are prepared to file your claim. You have exhausted all of your administrative remedies, (*in accordance with the Company manual.*) Still your case has not been rightfully resolved. Exhaust all in-house means before filing a complaint with the Department of
Fair Employment & Housing. With her attorney, she applied for a "Right-to-sue" notice. Review the application below to see what questions you will be asked if you have a case.

Carol D. Mitchell

SAMPLE LAST LETTER TO EMPLOYER
BEFORE FILING WITH OUTSIDE AGENCIES

<u>CERTIFIED MAIL/EMAIL</u>

XYZ Company   January 17, 20_____
Attn: President, Yoo
P.O. Box XXX
Los Angeles, California 90210

Dear Mr. Yoo:

I have completed the following actions in accordance with your grievance policy as stated on pages 35 & 36 of your *Employee Handbook*:

- ☐ I reported discrimination to my supervisor the day it happened on 11/30/03.
- ☐ On 12/18/04 I appropriately submitted your form #CS92-05 to Kathy Doe in the Department of Human Resources.
- ☐ On 12/07/05, I met with you. Then on 01/11/2005, (the date you said you would get back to me), I heard nothing from you. On that date, Kathy said you ended my employment without cause.

To date, I have followed your complaint process according to policy down to the letter. Still, my grievance has been overlooked and has not been settled.

I sincerely want to resolve these issues in house. Please contact me at 310-565-XXXX in five days to discuss resolution of the wrongful termination, loss of overtime wages and other employment issues. Otherwise, on January 24, 2005, I will carry my petition to the *Department of Labor* and the *Department of Fair **Employment & Housing** and the Equal Employment Opportunity Commission*, where I am sure I will get fair resolution of my discrimination issues and wage losses.

                                                            Very truly yours,

                                                            John X. Doe

Your Rights
Employment Guide

DFEH

H
☐ 1001 Tower Way, Suite 250
Bakersfield, CA
93309-1586
(661) 395-2729

C
☐
1320 East Shaw Avenue,
Suite #150
Fresno, CA 93710-7919
(559) 244-4760

B
☐
611 West Sixth Street,
Suite 1500
Los Angeles,
CA 90017-3116
(213) 439-6799

M

E
☐ 1515 Clay Street,
Suite #701
Oakland, CA 94612-2512
(510) 622-2941

2000 "O" Street, Suite #120

"RIGHT-TO-SUE-NOTICE" INSTRUCTIONS

You have requested a "right-to-sue notice" from the Department of Fair Employment and Housing. The Fair Employment and Housing Act (FEHA), at Government Code section 12965, subdivision (b), requires that individuals must exhaust their administrative remedies with the Department of Fair Employment and Housing (DFEH) by filing a complaint and obtaining a "right-to-sue notice" from the Department before filing a lawsuit under the **FEHA**. DFEH will accept requests for an immediate **DFEH** "right-to-sue notice" from persons who have decided to proceed in court. Your DFEH complaint must be filed within one year from the last act of discrimination or you may lose your right to file a lawsuit under the **FEHA**.

<u>The Process of proceeding directly to court without an investigation by DFEH is advisable only if you have an attorney. If you do not have an attorney, you can file a discrimination complaint with DFEH for investigation. If you decide to file a lawsuit later, you can still do so.</u> If you wish to have your complaint investigated by DFEH, call 1-800-884-1684 for an appointment.

If you receive an immediate **DFEH** "right-to-sue notice," your complaint **will not be investigated by DFEH even if you later decide not to file a lawsuit.**

If you receive an immediate **DFEH** "right-to-sue notice," **your complaint will not be dual-filed by DFEH with the U.S. Equal Employment Opportunity Commission (EEOC). DFEH complaints may be dual-filed with EEOC only if DFEH accepts the complaint**

Carol D. Mitchell

☐ J	Sacramento, CA 95814-5212 (916) 445-5523
☐ D	1845 S. Business Ctr. Dr., Suite #127 San Bernardino, CA 92408-3426 (909) 383-4373
☐ A	350 W. Ash Street, Suite 950 San Diego, CA 92101-3440 (610) 645-2681
☐ G	121 Spear Street, Suite #430 San Francisco, CA 94105-1581 (415) 904-2303
☐ K	111 North Market Street, Suite #810 San Jose, CA 95113-1102 (408) 277-1277
☐ L	2101 E. 4th Street, Suite

for investigation. In order to receive a federal right-to-sue notice, you must file a complaint with EEOC **WITHIN 30 days of your receipt of the DFEH "NOTICE OF CASE CLOSURE" OR WITHIN 300 DAYS OF THE ALLEGED DISCRIMINATORY ACT, WHICHEVER IS EARLIER.** The telephone number for EEOC in Northern California is (415) 356-5100. The Southern California EEOC telephone number is (213) 894-1000.

EEOC enforces laws which prohibit discrimination based on race, religion, color, sex, national origin, age (40 or over) or disability. For race, religion, color, sex, national origin and disability complaints, **EEOC** has jurisdiction over employers who employ 15 or more persons. For age complaints, **EEOC** has jurisdiction over employers who employ 20 or more persons.

In signing the enclosed documents, you are acknowledging the following:

1) You have read and understood this letter.

2) You understand that once **DFEH** has issued an authorization to file a lawsuit DFEH will not investigate or reopen your complaint. **Furthermore, you have chosen not to exercise your option of having DFEH investigate your complaint and of electing court action later. You also understand you should have an attorney to file a lawsuit.**

3) You understand that **DFEH** will not file your complaint with EEOC, and that if you wish to obtain a federal right-to-sue notice from EEOC you must contact EEOC directly.

4) You have one year form the date of the **DFEH** "right-to-sue notice"

Your Rights

Employment Guide

255-B
Santa Ana, CA 92705-3814
(714) 558-4266

1732 Palma Drive,
Suite 200
Ventura, CA 93003-5796
(805) 654-4514

to file a lawsuit.

If you wish to request an immediate DFEH "right-to-sue-notice" to file a lawsuit, complete the enclosed documents, and return them to the DFEH office checked in the margin of this letter. If you are filing against more than one Company or individual, you must submit a complaint form for each one. If there are not enough forms enclosed, please request additional copies from the office checked in the margin, or have additional copies made from the form enclosed. Please complete, sign and date, all of the complaint forms.

Carol D. Mitchell

CHAPTER 12
SAMPLE LETTERS

I wish to pursue this matter in court. I hereby request that the Department of Fair Employment and Housing provide a right-to-sue notice. I understand that if I want a federal notice Of right-to-sue, I must visit the U.S. Equal Employment Opportunity Commission (EEOC) to file a complaint within 30 days of receipt of the DFEH "Notice of Case Closure," or within 300 days of the alleged discriminatory act, whichever is earlier.

I have not been coerced into making this request, nor do I make it based on fear of retaliation if I do not do so. I understand it is the Department of Fair Employment and Housing's Policy to not process or reopen a complaint once the complaint has been closed on the basis of "Complainant Elected Court Action."

I declare under penalty of perjury under the laws of the State of California that the foregoing is true and correct of my own knowledge except as to matters stated on my Information and belief, and as to those matters I believe it to be true.

Dated _____

COMPLAINANT'S SIGNATURE

AT _____
CITY

Your Rights

Employment Guide

RIGHT-TO-SUE COMPLAINT INFORMATION SHEET

DFEH needs a separate signed complaint for each employer, person, labor organization, employment agency, apprenticeship committee, state or local
government agency you wish to file against. If you are filing against both a Company and an individual(s), please complete separate complaint forms naming
 the Company or an individual in the appropriate area.
Please complete the following so that DFEH can process your complaint and for DFEH for statistical purposes, and return with your signed complaint(s):

YOUR RACE:/ETHNICITY (Check one)
—African-American
—African - Other
—Asian/Pacific Islander (specify)_____
—Caucasian (Non-Hispanic)
—Native American
—Hispanic (specify) _____

YOUR PRIMARY LANGUAGE (specify)

_____

YOUR AGE:_____

IF FILING BECAUSE OF YOUR NATIONAL ORIGIN/ANCESTRY, YOUR NATIONAL (SPECIFY)

IF FILING BECAUSE OF SEX, THE REASON:
—Harassment
—Orientation
—Pregnancy
—Denied Right to Wear Pants
—Other Allegations (List)

YOUR GENDER:
—Female
—Male

YOUR OCCUPATION:
—Clerical
—Craft
—Equipment Operator
—Laborer
—Manager

Carol D. Mitchell

_____

IF FILING BECAUSE OF DISABILITY,
YOUR DISABILITY
—AIDS
—Blood/Circulation
—Brain/Nerves/Muscles
—Digestive/Urinary/Reproduction
—Hearing
—Heart
—Limbs (Arms/Legs)
—Mental
—Sight
—Speech/Respiratory
—Spinal/Back

IF FILING BECAUSE OF MARITAL STATUS
YOUR MARITAL STATUS: (check one)
—Cohabitation
—Divorced
—Married
—Single

IF FILING BECAUSE OF RELIGION,
YOUR RELIGION: (specify)
_____

—Paraprofessional
—Professional
—Sales
—Service
—Supervisor
—Technician

HOW YOU HEARD ABOUT DFEH:
—Attorney
—Bus/BART Advertisement
—Community Organization
—EEOC
—EDD
—Friend
—Human Relations Commission
—Labor Standards Enforcement
—Local Government Agency
—Poster
—Prior Contact with DFEH
—Radio
—Telephone Book
—TV
—DFEH Web Site

DO YOU HAVE AN ATTORNEY?
—Yes   —No
_____ Your Signature

The Fair Employment and Housing Act (FEHA), at Government Code section 12965,

Your Rights

Employment Guide

Subdivision (b), requires that individuals must exhaust their administrative remedies with the Department of Fair Employment and Housing (DFEH) by filing a complaint and obtaining a "right-to-sue notice" from the Department before filing a lawsuit under the FEHA. DFEH will accept requests for an immediate DFEH "right-to-sue notice" from persons who have decided to proceed in court. Your complaint must be filed within one year from the last act of discrimination or you may lose your right to file a lawsuit under the FEHA:

STATE OF CALIFORNIA
STATE AND CONSUMER SERVICES AGENCY
DEPARTMENT OF FAIR EMPLOYMENT AND HOUSING

FOR OFFICIAL USE ONLY

Interview Date:	Processing Time: :HR :MIN
Approval:	Action Taken:
Interviewer:	Computer Entry:

PRE-COMPLAINT QUESTIONNAIRE - EMPLOYMENT

The information requested on this form will assist the Department in helping you. There is no guarantee that the information submitted will result in an investigation. Please check or answer only those questions that apply.

PLEASE PRINT   DATE _____

NAME _____
         First   Middle   Last
ADDRESS _____
         Street   Apt. Number   City   County   ZIP Code
TELEPHONE NUMBER: WORK ( ) _____ HOME ( ) _____
                             Area Code   Area Code
I prefer to be contacted by telephone at work/home: Days: _____   Time: _____

Person to contact if you cannot be reached or if you move:
Name _____ TELEPHONE ( ) _____
                                                                Area Code

I WISH TO COMPLAIN AGAINST: (Name and address of company, government entity [city, county, state], employment agency, union, etc.)

NAME _____

ADDRESS _____
         Street   City   County   ZIP Code
TELEPHONE NUMBER: WORK ( ) _____   NUMBER OF EMPLOYEES (Estimate, if necessary)
                           Area Code   Job Site _____ Company-Wide _____

I WISH TO COMPLAIN AGAINST: (Other named individuals who were involved in this particular complaint.)
NAME _____
TITLE _____ TELEPHONE ( ) _____
                                                                Area Code
ADDRESS _____
         (if known)   Street   City   County   ZIP Code
EMPLOYER LISTED ON W-2 FORM:
NAME _____
ADDRESS _____
         (if known)   Street   City   County   ZIP Code

(CONTINUE ON BACK IF NECESSARY)

1. I believe I was discriminated against because of my (please circle):

   ❏ Race   ❏ Sex   ❏ Cancer   ❏ Pregnancy   ❏ Age (40 and over)
   ❏ Color   ❏ Sexual Orientation   ❏ Genetic   ❏ Marital Status   ❏ Denial of Family Care
                                                  Characterisitcs   Leave
   ❏ Religion _____   ❏ Disability (including AIDS) _____   ❏ National Origin/Ancestry _____
             (Please specify)   (Please specify)   (Please specify)

2. Circle the discriminatory treatment and indicate the *date occurred*:

   Terminated/Laid Off _____   Not Hired _____   Denied Promotion _____   Harassed _____
   Denied Leave (Pregnancy/Family Care Leave) _____   Denied Accommodation _____   Denied Equal Pay _____
   Denied Accommodation for Pregnancy _____   Impermissible Non-Job-Related Inquiry _____
   Retaliation _____   Other _____

DFEH-600-03I (06/03)

American LegalNet, Inc.
www.FormsWorkflow.com

Your Rights

Employment Guide

DEPARTMENT OF FAIR EMPLOYMENT & HOUSING
1001 Tower Way, Suite #250
Bakersfield, CA 93309-1586
(661) 395-2729

DEPARTMENT OF FAIR EMPLOYMENT & HOUSING
1320 E. Shaw Avenue, Suite #150
Fresno, CA 93710-7979
(559) 244-4760

DEPARTMENT OF FAIR EMPLOYMENT & HOUSING
611 West Sixth Street, Suite #1500
Los Angeles, CA 90017-3116
(213) 439-6799

DEPARTMENT OF FAIR EMPLOYMENT & HOUSING
1515 Clay Street, Suite #701
Oakland, CA 94612-2512
(510) 622-2941

DEPARTMENT OF FAIR EMPLOYMENT & HOUSING
2000 "O" Street, Suite #120
Sacramento, CA 95814-5212
(916) 445-5523

DEPARTMENT OF FAIR EMPLOYMENT & HOUSING 1845 S. Business Center Drive, Suite #127
San Bernardino, CA 92408-3426
(909) 383-4373

DEPARTMENT OF FAIR EMPLOYMENT & HOUSING
350 W. Ash Street, Suite #950
San Diego, CA 92101-3440
(619) 645-2681

DEPARTMENT OF FAIR EMPLOYMENT & HOUSING
121 Spear Street, Suite #430
San Francisco, CA 94105-1581
(415) 904-2303

DEPARTMENT OF FAIR EMPLOYMENT & HOUSING
111 North Market Street, Suite #810

DEPARTMENT OF FAIR EMPLOYMENT & HOUSING
2101 East 4th Street, Suite #255-B

Carol D. Mitchell

San Jose, CA 95113-1102
(408) 277-1277

Santa Ana, CA 92705-3814
(714) 558-4266

DEPARTMENT OF FAIR EMPLOYMENT & HOUSING
1732 Palma Drive, Suite #200
Ventura, CA 93003-5796
(805) 654-4514

DEPARTMENT OF FAIR EMPLOYMENT & HOUSING
TTY (1-800) 700-2320

Your Rights
Employment Guide

Chapter 13
50 Fastest Growing Industries

Top 50 Fastest-Growing Industries
Displaying Records 1 - 25 of 50 Next 25 > Show All Records

#	Industry	Employment 2006	Employment 2016	Percent Change
1	Management, scientific, and technical consulting services	920,900	1,638,700	78%
2	Services for the elderly and persons with disabilities	493,400	860,400	74%
3	Gambling industries	137,000	227,300	66%
4	Home health care services	867,100	1,347,600	55%
5	Educational support services, public and private	90,800	138,600	53%
6	Community care facilities for the elderly	639,400	960,100	50%
7	Other financial investment activities	306,600	449,500	47%
8	Facilities support services	122,800	179,100	46%
9	Securities and commodity contracts, brokerages, and exchanges	509,700	742,900	46%
10	Internet publishing and broadcasting	34,500	49,700	44%
11	Other investment pools and funds	45,000	63,900	42%

Carol D. Mitchell

#	Industry	Employment 2006	Employment 2016	Percent Change
12	All other ambulatory health care services	86,500	121,900	41%
13	Wireless telecommunications carriers (except satellite)	200,100	281,900	41%
14	Other automotive repair and maintenance	229,000	322,100	41%
15	Independent artists, writers, and performers	46,800	64,800	38%
16	Computer systems design and related services	1,278,200	1,767,600	38%
17	Residential mental health and substance abuse facilities	165,900	229,100	38%
18	Cable and other program distribution	144,300	197,800	37%
19	Museums, historical sites, and similar institutions	123,900	167,400	35%
20	Specialty (except psychiatric and substance abuse) hospitals, public and private	197,200	265,000	34%
21	Child day care services	806,700	1,078,400	34%
22	Veterinary services	278,000	371,000	33%
23	Data processing, hosting, and related services	261,600	348,000	33%
24	Other schools and instruction, public and private	285,100	379,200	33%
25	Fitness and recreational sports centers	507,000	672,700	33%

Your Rights

Employment Guide

Top 50 Industries with the Largest Employment

2	General medical and surgical hospitals, public and private	4,988,300
3	Full-service restaurants	4,447,000
4	Limited-service eating places	4,018,700
5	Employment services	3,656,600
6	Colleges, universities, and professional schools, public and private	3,433,900
7	Grocery stores	2,462,600
8	Offices of physicians	2,153,600
9	Management of companies and enterprises	1,809,400
10	Depository credit intermediation	1,803,200
11	Religious organizations	1,665,900
12	Nursing care facilities	1,584,200
13	Department stores	1,550,900
14	Other general merchandise stores	1,362,000
15	Computer systems design and related services	1,278,200
16	Automobile dealers	1,246,700
17	Building material and supplies dealers	1,176,100
18	Legal services	1,173,400
19	Clothing stores	1,090,400
20	Residential building construction	1,017,500

Carol D. Mitchell

21	General freight trucking	1,003,900
22	Plumbing, heating, and air-conditioning contractors	982,500
23	Management, scientific, and technical consulting services	920,900
24	Electrical contractors	903,700
25	Accounting, tax preparation, bookkeeping, and payroll services	889,300

25 HIGHEST PAYING JOBS

Top 50 Highest-Paying Industries by Average Weekly Wages
Displaying Records 1-25 of 50

1	Cigarette Manufacturing	$1,992	$103,599
2	Coal and Other Mineral and Ore Merchant Wholesalers	$1,729	$89,903
3	Commodity Contracts Brokerage	$2,646	$137,592
4	Commodity Contracts Dealing	$3,089	$160,638
5	Computer and Computer Peripheral Equipment and Software Merchant Wholesalers	$1,899	$98,755
6	Computer Storage Device Manufacturing	$1,827	$95,021
7	Computer Terminal Manufacturing	$2,026	$105,365
8	Crude Petroleum and Natural Gas Extraction	$2,525	$131,281
9	Deep Sea Freight Transportation	$1,802	$93,703
10	Electronic Computer Manufacturing	$2,620	$136,224
11	Flavoring Syrup and Concentrate Manufacturing	$1,949	$101,368
12	Guided Missile and Space Vehicle Manufacturing	$1,883	$97,891
13	House Slipper Manufacturing	$1,667	$86,686

Your Rights

Employment Guide

14	Independent Artists, Writers, and Performers	$2,137	$111,139
15	Instrument Manufacturing for Measuring and Testing Electricity and Electrical Signals	$1,766	$91,832
16	Integrated Record Production/Distribution	$2,259	$117,482
17	International Trade Financing	$2,502	$130,082
18	Internet Publishing and Broadcasting	$1,682	$87,426
19	Internet Service Providers	$1,650	$85,792
20	Investment Advice	$2,080	$108,136
21	Investment Banking and Securities Dealing	$2,807	$145,973
22	Miscellaneous Financial Investment Activities	$2,489	$129,407
23	Miscellaneous Intermediation	$3,103	$161,368
24	Natural Gas Liquid Extraction	$2,443	$127,014
25	News Syndicates	$1,661	$86,346

Carol D. Mitchell

LATEST MAIL TRENDS

The Mail

When you are serious about your business, save yourself the time of screwing things up with a million and one mail options. Federal Express, Airborne, UPS and companies like them do a great job of picking up and delivering your mail. However, it does not get any better than the great *United States Post Office*. When you really want to do it right, consider the following trademark mailing options:

Your Rights

Employment Guide

Mail Trends Continued
For The Smart Worker

Resource: http://www.coupondeals.us/shipping/tracking.php

Tracking Phone Numbers and Websites

UPS Package Tracking

Phone: 1-800-742-5877

FedEx Package Tracking

Phone: 1-800-463-3339

U.S. Postal Service Package Tracking: Priority Mail

Airborne Express and DHL have been merged.

DHL Worldwide Express Package Tracking

Phone: 1-800-225-5345 (U.S. customers only)

Please note: Package tracking services are not available for DHL World Mail shipments, as these are delivered by air mail to the destination country/continent and then handled by the local postal system.

A1 Courier Services Package Tracking

ABF Freight System, Inc. Package Tracking

Phone: 1-800-610-5544

Dynamex Package Tracking

Phone: 1-206-574-7180

Carol D. Mitchell

Eagle Package Tracking
Phone: 1-800-888-4949

Enroute Package Tracking
Phone: 1-800-560-5488

Menlo Worldwide/UPS Supply Chain Solutions Package Tracking
Phone: 1-800-443-6379

Roadway Express Tracking Package Tracking
Phone: 1-888-550-9800

Your Rights

Employment Guide

STATE OF CALIFORNIA
Department of Industrial Relations
<u>Division of Labor Standards Enforcement</u>

You have kept all of your time cards and hand-sheets. You have been a good employee who still has not been paid all of your due wages. You have approached and handled every facet of your business seriously, with dignity. Well, you need to know how the process of the Labor Department works. Before you read on remember the tip of this chapter: ***"Be calm, cool and collective always"****.* You are intelligent; you are exercising your rights and you simply want to get what is yours. Payroll denied your claim. But, you know you are right. Therefore, at each interval in dealing with what is owed to you, you mailed certified letters and you can prove to the judge with your receipts, notes and written evidence that you do things in an orderly fashion. You kept your receipts. You put the cost, time and dates of those receipts in your diary, and the judge is going to put weight on your orderly stratagem. You know your rights and now you need to get the money your employer owes you and you are serious.

Why you are going to the Department of Labor

- You have wages or overtime that is due to you that has not been paid.
- *http://www.leginfo.ca.gov/cgi-bin/calawquery?codesection=lab&codebody=&hits=20*
- *Your Labor Resource Connection*
- You have reported this to your immediate supervisor/nothing was done.
- You have reported this to your supervisor's boss and nothing was done.
- You have appealed to each and every chain of command in your Company/nothing was done.
- You have gone through the employee handbook a dozen times. You still have not been paid. No matter what the handbook says, all time worked MUST BE PAID. Never let the employer convince you that hours worked are not compensable.

Good for you! You needed to know - now you are ready to take this job to the Labor Board - please read the following and good luck!

Carol D. Mitchell

EMPLOYEE LABOR CLAIMS CODES

- Unpaid wages (including commissions and bonuses) - Labor Code §§ 200, 201, and 202
- **California LABOR CODE SECTION 1171-1205**
- Wages paid by check issued with insufficient funds - Labor Code § 212
- Final paycheck not received - Labor Code §§ 201, 202, and 203
- Unused vacation hours which were not paid - Labor Code 227.3
- Unauthorized deductions from paychecks - Labor Code §§ 221 and 224
- Unpaid expenses - Labor Code § 2802
- Reinstatement and/or back wages as a result of discrimination - Labor Code § 98.7 (c)

For a listing of the types of complaints, which can be filed with this office, contact the Public Information Unit to request a list.

ANY EMPLOYEE, FORMER EMPLOYEE, OR GROUP OF EMPLOYEES MAY FILE A GENERAL CLAIM <u>TO REPORT THE FOLLOWING</u>:

- Failure of employer to issue written wage deduction statements - Labor Code § 226, IWC Orders
- Violations of garment manufacturing laws - Labor Code §§ 2670-2681
- Violations of child labor laws Labor Code §§ 1285-1384
- Violations of farm labor laws Labor Code §§1682-1698.7
- Failure to have workers' compensation insurance §§-Labor Code § 3700
- Violations of wage and hour laws - Labor Code §§500-558, IWC Orders
- Payment of prevailing wages on public works projects - Labor Code §§ 1775

WHAT IS THE TIME PERIOD FOR FILING A CLAIM?

A claim based on an oral agreement must be filed within 2 years or within 4 years if based on a written agreement. A claim for unpaid overtime or minimum wages must be filed within three years. (Code of Civil Procedure § 338) Discrimination complaints must be filed within 6 months of termination or other discriminatory acts. (Labor Code § 98.7 (a)] However, it is recommended that you file as soon as possible.

Your Rights
Employment Guide

WHERE DO I FILE

All information should be completed on the claim form to avoid delay in the claim process. Copies of any documents you have to support your claim should be attached to your claim form.

WHAT HAPPENS NEXT

Once you have submitted your claim form, you will be contacted by mail and provided the name and telephone number of the representative handling your claim. For additional information, refer to the pamphlet titled: ***"Policies and Procedures for Wage Claim Processing"***.

Carol D. Mitchell

CHAPTER 14

DIVISION OF LABOR STANDARDS LOCATIONS

DIVISION OF LABOR STANDARDS ENFORCEMENT 5555 California Avenue, Suite #200 Bakersfield, California 93309 **(661) 395-2710**	**DIVISION OF LABOR STANDARDS ENFORCEMENT** 464 West 4th Street, Room 348 San Bernardino, California 92401 **(909) 383-4333**
DIVISION OF LABOR STANDARDS ENFORCEMENT 619 Second Street, Room 109 Eureka, California 95501 **(707) 445-6613**	**DIVISION OF LABOR STANDARDS ENFORCEMENT** 7575 Metropolitan, Room 210 San Diego, California 92123 **(619) 220-5457**
DIVISION OF LABOR STANDARDS ENFORCEMENT 770 East Shaw Avenue, Suite #315 Fresno, California 93710 **(559) 244-5340**	**DIVISION OF LABOR STANDARDS ENFORCEMENT** 455 Golden Gate Avenue, 8th Floor San Francisco, California 94102 **(415) 421-6272**
DIVISION OF LABOR STANDARDS ENFORCEMENT 300 Ocean gate, 3rd Floor Long Beach, California 90802 **(562) 590-5048**	**DIVISION OF LABOR STANDARDS ENFORCEMENT** 100 Paseo de San Antonio, Room 120 San Jose, California 95113 **(408) 277-1266**

Your Rights

Employment Guide

DIVISION OF LABOR STANDARDS ENFORCEMENT 320 W. Fourth Street, Suite #450 Los Angeles, California 90013 **(213) 620-6330**	**DIVISION OF LABOR STANDARDS ENFORCEMENT** 28 Civic Center Plaza, Room 625 Santa Ana, California 92701 **(714) 558-4910**
DIVISION OF LABOR STANDARDS ENFORCEMENT 1515 Clay Street, Room 801 Oakland, California 94612 **(510) 622-3273**	**DIVISION OF LABOR STANDARDS ENFORCEMENT** 411 East Canon Perdido, Room 3 Santa Barbara, California 93101 **(805) 568-1222**
DIVISION OF LABOR STANDARDS ENFORCEMENT 2115 Civic Center Drive, #17 Redding, California 96001 **(530) 225-2655**	DIVISION OF LABOR STANDARDS ENFORCEMENT 50 "D" Street, Suite #360 Santa Rosa, California 95404 **(707) 576-2362**
DIVISION OF LABOR STANDARDS ENFORCEMENT 2031 Howe Avenue, Suite #100 Sacramento, California 95825 **(916) 263-1811**	**DIVISION OF LABOR STANDARDS ENFORCEMENT** 31 East Channel Street, Room 317 Stockton, California 95202 **(209) 948-7770**
Division of Labor Standards Enforcement 1870 N. Main Street, Suite #150 Salinas, California 93906 **(909) 383-4334**	**Division of Labor Standards Enforcement** 6150 Van Nuys Boulevard, Room #206 Van Nuys, California 91401 **(831) 443-3041**

SAMPLE SETTLEMENT LETTER TO THE DEPARTMENT OF LABOR

LABOR COMMISSIONER, STATE OF CALIFORNIA
Department of Industrial Relations
Division of Labor Standards Enforcement
455 Golden Gate Avenue - 8th Floor East
San Francisco, CA 94102
Telephone: (415) 703-5300 Fax: (415) 703-4130
Tuesday, April 26, 2_____

SETTLEMENT AGREEMENT
Regarding Overtime Between

Claimant: JANE DOE

Defendant: CORPORATE MANAGEMENT COMPANY CORPORATION

RE: **CASE NUMBER: 11-30777 LK - COMPLAIN**

> Overtime wages for hours more than 8 (8) per day or 40 per week for the period 11/22/2--- through 12/09/2004, being 28 hours at:
> $18.75 per hour = $525.00;
> Plus 1 hour at $25.00 per hour = $25.00
> TOTALING: $550.00

Dear Corporate Management Company & Labor Commissioner, My name is Jane Doe. I am the Claimant in the aforementioned **CASE NO. 11-30777**. I have agreed to accept a check from Corporate Management Company Corporation for $550.00 to SETTLE MY OVERTIME WAGE DISPUTE that was filed on January 19, 2003 and was heard in your office on April 25, 2003. We have agreed to SETTLE in the full and total amount of $550.00. I agree with this settlement, which is the reason that I am writing this letter to you. Upon receipt of this payment, there are no further wage issues with Corporate Management Company Corporation.

Your Rights Employment Guide

THE SAMPLE DECLARATION OF JANE DOE'S EYE WITNESS

JANE DOE'S WITNESS
Telephone: 510-000-0000
Telephone: 707-000-0000

DECLARATION OF JANE DOE'S WITNESS

JANE DOE'S WITNESS, Declares As Follows:

(1.) I am above the age of eighteen years old. I am not a party to this action, and if called upon to testify in open court, I would testify as follows:

(2.) I am a resident of the State of California, City of Claremont, California

(3.) I am aware that Jane Doe worked overtime on November 30, 2003. Jane Doe was new to this job, she was scared and she told me many times that she felt that she had no choice but to work overtime in order to keep her job. I saw Jane Doe working overtime. I witnessed the anxiety Ms. Doe suffered on this job because of the stress of not getting paid her overtime.

Carol D. Mitchell

Pursuant to the laws of the State of California and under penalty of perjury, I hereby declare that the foregoing is true and correct to the best of my memory and recollection

THE SAMPLE DEMAND LETTER

May 6, 2_____

XYZ Company
Attn: Department of Human Resources
1258 Employment Drive
Pomona, CA 91768
RE: E<small>MPLOYMENT</small> D<small>ISCRIMINATION</small>, 02/12/2__
Dear Department of Human Resources:

    Per our discussion, please review the attached e-mail sent to me by a witness with no interest in my case, who was also discriminated against by Guy B at XYZ Company in Pomona, CA as I was. Please review the attached letter and the initial itemization of all incidences of harassment and all expenses that were submitted to your legal department for denouement of this employment conflict.

    Before going to the Department of Fair Employment & Housing, I would like to initiate a chance to settle the case with you. I believe that the full and total sum of *$10,000.00* would be an equitable and fair settlement amount for all that I have suffered, *(see attached itemized list)* and to cover outstanding medical cost as has

Carol Denise Mitchell

Your Rights Employment Guide

been itemized specifically on my list. In order to cure this situation and put it all behind me I pray that we can handle Continued…

    this employment matter out of court. Therefore, I sincerely hope that this faxed proposal for settlement will be agreeable to XYZ Company, and to the Department of Human Resources, and your legal department. If not, I have no other choice but to have a lawyer pursue this case further.

    Your expeditious reply to this *Settlement Proposal* is greatly appreciated. Should I not hear from you in ten (10) working business days, then I will have no choice but to pursue and implement all my legal options fully.

Sincerely,

Jane Doe
P.O. Box XXX
Pomona, CA 91768

Carol D. Mitchell

Chapter 15
Workers Compensation

Employee Guide to Worker's Compensation
Note: *Always Reference Current Workers Compensation Law*

You were hurt on the job. You are not sure what workers compensation is. Here is what you should do:

FIRST: Know that workers compensation is the insurance that the law requires your employer to have to help you when you get hurt on the job, or if you get sick because of your job.

REPORT: As soon as you get hurt on the job, (*no matter how minor you think that the injury is*) tell your supervisor that you have been hurt. Don't worry about how big or small the injury is report it, and the doctor appointed to treat you will diagnose your injury appropriately. If you are hurt on the job and no one is around call 911. Make sure you tell the emergency staff that your injury is a job related injury.

What happens next?

    A. Next, your employer will give you a claim form.

B. Make sure the form is called: The Workers Compensation (**DWC 1**) see image below
C. Be sure and ask for the above form!
D. When you get the form complete the "Employee" section (only)
E. Give your completed (DWC1) form to your employer.

Carol D. Mitchell

- F. Keep a copy of this form until you get the signed and dated copy from your employer.
- G. Make sure your injury is recorded on the 301 Form for your individual injury and make sure the manager updates all the appropriate logs.
- H. Know: The Division of Workers Compensation **#1-800-736-7401**

What are my rights?

- A. One day after you file a claim form, the law requires the employer to authorize medical treatment as required and limited by the law, until the claim is accepted or rejected.
- B. You have a limit of $10,000.00 total.
- C. If your claim is rejected, get a workers compensation attorney immediately!

How long do I have to file a claim?

- A. You should tell your employer within 30 days of the date of injury.

- B. REMEMBER: you should always act quickly so as not to risk losing your benefits because you waited too long to report your injury.

If you are injured on the job, chances are you are going to be confused by the complicated process of Workers Compensation

Your Rights
Employment Guide

law. You are going to want to know what the process is. Even if your injury was a total accident, chances are after you get hurt on the job your relationship at work will change. One way or another it will not be the same. Workers who are hurt are sometimes confused by the procedures.

Be sure: That you have a case and pursue your benefits fully. Look in the yellow pages for a Workers Compensation attorney. Familiarize your-self with each detail of what your case entails:

- **Temporary Disability**

TD is paid at a weekly rate during the time the doctor says that the injured worker is unable to work because of the injury. TD is paid at the rate of two-thirds (66%) of the injured employees gross earnings up to the maximum that is set by law. The maximum rate for Temporary Disability is presently paid at the rate of $490.00 a week, *(see chart on the next page for additional rates)* for injuries that have occurred on or after January 01, 1996. Wait for first check: two-weeks.

- **Permanent Disability**

For workers left with any residual disability they may be entitled to receive a *permanent disability award*. These monies are not payable until the medical condition becomes permanent and stationary, which means the physician has signed off on the condition as having been leveled off and will stay substantially the same in the future. Remember: If the doctor says there has been a total recovery, there would be no permanent disability award.

> **Note:** *When dealing with Workers Compensation issues and or injuries, be smart. What may not hurt today may sear tomorrow. If injured on the job, always negotiate for future medical awards for your injury where it is warranted.*

- **Medical Consultation**

When the doctor ends your treatment and says that your medical condition may be permanent and stationary or that you can go back to work, get examined by a Qualified Medical Examiner. If you are not represented by an attorney, the insurance Company will send you the injured party, a list of doctors, (QME) to choose from. If you, the injured worker have a lawyer, your lawyer will choose the QME or make an agreement with the insurance Company to utilize QME.

Your Rights
Employment Guide

- **Settlement of the Case**

When all the medical reports are submitted with a detail narrative including professional opinions by all of your treating doctors, you may be ready to settle your case. The report will be rated and a percentage of disability will be assigned to the doctors opinions in accordance with the rating guidelines of the State of California. The rating percentage is then converted into a monetary settlement amount and all ratings and preset rating guidelines are arranged in accordance with a schedule.

> **Note:** *If you have been without an attorney before; now is the time to hire one. You will receive more of the benefits you deserve if you have an experienced lawyer to negotiate your case for you. Consult the State of California Bar Association or your yellow pages for a Workers Compensation Attorney.*

- **Rehabilitation**

If you are not able to return to the job you had when you got injured; you may be eligible for rehabilitation. While you are pursuing rehabilitation training you will continue to receive either temporary disability benefits or a rehabilitation maintenance allowance.

Workers' Compensation Appeals Board

The Workers' Compensation Appeals Board is the state court for

Carol D. Mitchell

all industrial injuries involving your employer. The proceedings are administrative and there are not juries. Contact an office in your city for more information regarding your rights in Civil Court.

Important Points to Remember

If you are hurt on the job, no matter how minor it is, report it <u>immediately,</u> and demand, to see a doctor right away. An injury or illness that takes place due to your job is a workers' compensation injury or illness. If somebody tells you, "well, you picked up that box the wrong way! Had you picked it up right, you would not have gotten hurt." Say thank you to that person, then march right over to the telephone, call the HR person, tell them that you were hurt, and tell them to please send you all forms from BC to present for your injury. If there are witnesses that saw you get hurt <u>never,</u> feel embarrassed to write that person's name down or ask them to sign a declaration, and look up at the clock and right down the time you were hurt.

Your Rights
Employment Guide

If they don't testify today because of fear, or out of losing their job; believe me, they will have to talk when you subpoena them later to me to the Worker's Compensation Appeals Board for adjudication of your claim. Honest employers recognize injuries, and they process such matters accordingly. But, remember:

"If you get hurt on the job, no matter how minor, tell somebody immediately."

Workers Compensation Attorneys are very busy. Your case is important to them. Therefore, please be considerate and keep in mind before calling about your case incessantly, see if you can handle some questions yourself first.

<u>WHAT YOUR WORKERS COMPENSATION ATTORNEY *MIGHT* WANT YOU TO KNOW</u>

- I may not always be readily available
- You are not my only client
- I am at the board, a hearing or a conference OR adjudicating another case
- Your case is complicated to you; but, not to me
- You can call the insurance company yourself about your check
- You can call the insurance company yourself to change a doctor's appointment

Carol D. Mitchell

- Call doctors (directly) to change appointment dates/times
- Do not sign anything without my advice

Note: *The information provided here is current. Laws change all of the time, so keep abreast of*
   New Workers Compensation Laws and pay rates.

Worker's Compensation News!

Provides for $250,000 in death benefits to the estate of a deceased police officer who has no total dependents and no partial dependents for injuries occurring on or after January 1, 2003, but before January 1, 2004. **Worker's Compensation News!** Extends indefinitely the authority of a nurse practitioner or physician's assistant to provide workers' compensation medical treatment, prepare the doctor's first report and authorize up to 3 days off work if working under the supervision of a physician.

AB2866 Workers' Comp requires the Department of Insurance to post on its Internet site information for each person, association or business convicted of an insurance fraud violation involving workers' compensation insurance, services, or benefits. The information is to remain posted for a period of five years from the date of conviction or until the department is notified in writing by the person that the conviction has been reversed or expunged. SB899 Workers' Comp Starting August 1, 2004, new postings and pamphlets are required for the new workers' compensation law.

Your Rights

Employment Guide

WHAT'S NEW IN WORKERS COMPENSATION

DWC Initiates Procedure to Assess Administrative Penalties for Failure to Submit IMR Medical Records. The Division of Workers' Compensation (DWC) will initiate the procedure to assess
administrative penalties for claims administrator failure to timely submit relevant medical records in cases currently pending Independent Medical Review (IMR).Under Labor Code section 4610.5(i), DWC is authorized to assess penalties against claim administrators whose conduct has the effect of delaying the IMR process. Under current regulations, Maximus Federal Services, Inc., the organization designated by DWC to conduct IMR reviews, sends the claims administrator a Notice of Assignment
and Request for Information (NOARFI) in an IMR case. The notice advises of the relevant medical records to be submitted, which must be provided to Maximus within 15 days of the date on the NOARFI. The regulatory requirements for submitting records can be found at California Code of Regulations, title 8, section 9792.10.5.

Under California Code of Regulations, title 8, section 9792.12(c)(6), failure to submit the records within those 15 days will subject a claims administrator to an administrative
penalty of $500 for each day the records are untimely, up to a

Carol D. Mitchell

maximum of $5,000. DWC will send an Order to Show Cause to claims administrators who may be liable for a penalty, with the facts upon which the penalty is based, the penalty amount, and the administrative process for contesting a penalty.

The procedure to assess administrative penalties will commence in cases where there is a failure to timely submit medical records dated on and after December 1, 2014. For IMR cases currently pending at Maximus as of December 1, 2014, the penalty procedure will commence if the relevant medical records are not received on or before December 15, 2014. DWC will continue to post updates and notifications regarding the IMR system on the

Your Rights

Employment Guide

DIVISION OF WORKERS COMPENSATION

INFORMATION/ASSISTANCE OFFICERS Anaheim 714-738-4038	INFORMATION/ASSISTANCE OFFICERS Bakersfield 661-395-2514
INFORMATION/ASSISTANCE OFFICERS Eureka 707-441-5723	INFORMATION/ASSISTANCE OFFICERS Fresno 559-445-5355
INFORMATION/ASSISTANCE OFFICERS Goleta 805-968-4158	INFORMATION/ASSISTANCE OFFICERS Grover Beach 805-481-3380
INFORMATION/ASSISTANCE OFFICERS Long Beach 562-590-5240	INFORMATION/ASSISTANCE OFFICERS Los Angeles 213-576-7389
INFORMATION/ASSISTANCE OFFICERS Oakland 510-622-2861 408-277-1277	INFORMATION/ASSISTANCE OFFICERS Oxnard 805-485-3528 714-558-4266
INFORMATION/ASSISTANCE OFFICERS Pomona 909-623-8568	INFORMATION/ASSISTANCE OFFICERS Redding 530-225-2047

Carol D. Mitchell

STATEWIDE INFORMATION OFFICERS

INFORMATION/ASSISTANCE OFFICERS	INFORMATION/ASSISTANCE OFFICERS
Riverside 909-782-4347	Sacramento 916-263-2741
Salinas 831-443-3058	San Bernardino 909-383-4522
San Diego 619-767-2082	San Francisco 415-703-5020
San Jose 408-277-1292	Santa Ana 714-558-4597
Santa Monica 310-452-1188	Santa Rosa 707-576-2452
Stockton 209-948-7980	Van Nuys 818-901-5374

Your Rights

Employment Guide

Workers Compensation Nationwide Contacts

Division of Federal Employees' Compensation (DFEC)

Resource:
http://www.dol.gov/esa/owcp/dfec/regs/compliance/wc.htm

State Workers' Compensation Officials

Scroll down this page until you locate the appropriate state. Note that all states and territories are linked to their respective workers' compensation webpage.

Carol D. Mitchell

ALABAMA
Scottie Spates, Director
Department of Industrial Relations
Workers' Compensation Division
649 Monroe Street
Montgomery, AL 36131
(334) 353-0990 or 1-800-528-5166
(Contact: Teresa Davis)

ALASKA
Paul F. Lisankie, Director
Department of Labor
Workers' Compensation Division
1111 West 8th Street, Room 307
P. O. Box 115512
Juneau, AK 99811-5512
(907) 465-2790

ARIZONA
Larry J. Etchechury, Director
Industrial Commission
800 West Washington Street
P. O. Box 19070
Phoenix, AZ 85007
(602) 542-4411 or 1-800-544-6488 (in-state calls only)

ARKANSAS
Butch Reeves, Chairman
Workers' Compensation Commission
324 Spring Street
P. O. Box 950
Little Rock, AR 72203-0950
(501) 682-3930 or 1-800-622-4472

CALIFORNIA
Carrie Nevans, Administrative Director
Division of Workers' Compensation
455 Golden Gate Avenue, 2nd Fl.
San Francisco, CA 94102-7014
(415) 703-5011 or 1-800-736-7401

COLORADO
Bob Summers, Director
Division of Workers' Compensation
633 17th Street, Suite 400
Denver, CO 80202
(303) 318-8700 or 1-888-390-7936
(Contact: JoAnne Allen Ibarra)

Your Rights

Employment Guide

CONNECTICUT
John A. Mastropietro,
Chairman
Workers'
Compensation
Commission
21 Oak Street
Hartford, CT 06106
(860) 493-1500 or 1-800-223-9675
(Contact: Peter Miecznikowski)

DELAWARE
John Kirk III,
Administrator
Office of Workers'
Compensation
4425 N. Market
Street, 3rd Floor
Wilmington, DE 19802
(302) 761-8200

DISTRICT OF COLUMBIA
James Jacobs,
Director
Office of Workers'
Compensation
64 New York
Avenue, N.E., 2nd Fl.
Washington, DC 20002
(202) 671-1050 (Ann Jelani

FLORIDA
Tanner Holloman,
Director
Division of Workers'
Compensation
200 East Gaines Street
Tallahassee, FL 32399-4220
(850) 413-1601 or 1-800-342-1741
(Contact: Duncan Hoehn)

GEORGIA
Carolyn Hall,
Chairman
Board of Workers'
Compensation
270 Peachtree Street, NW
Atlanta, GA 30303-1299
(404) 656-3875 or 1-800-533-0682
(Contact: Stan Carter)

HAWAII
Department of Labor
and Industrial
Relations
Disability
Compensation
Division
Princess Keelikolani
Building
830 Punchbowl
Street, Room 211
P. O. Box 3769
Honolulu, HI 96813
(808) 586-9161
(Contact: Clyde Imada)

Carol D. Mitchell

IDAHO
R.D. Maynard, Chairman
Industrial Commission
317 Main Street
P. O. Box 83720
Boise, ID 83720-0041
(208) 334-6000 or 1-800-950-2110
(Contact Nancy Breeson)

ILLINOIS
Amy J. Masters, Chairman
Illinois Workers' Compensation Commission
100 West Randolph Street
Suite 8-200
Chicago, IL 60601
(312) 814-6611

INDIANA
Linda Hamilton, Chairman
Workers' Compensation Board
402 West Washington Street, Room W-196
Indianapolis, IN 46204
(317) 232-3808 or 1-800-824-2667
(Contact Kristen)

IOWA
Christopher Godfrey, W.C. Commissioner
Div. of Workers' Compensation
Workforce Development Dept.
1000 East Grand Avenue
Des Moines, IA 50319-0209
(515) 281-5387 or 1-800-562-4692
(Contact: Sharon Ortega)

KANSAS
Paula Greathouse, Director
Division of Workers' Compensation
800 SW Jackson Street, 7th Floor
Topeka, KS 66612-1227
(785) 296-2996 or 1-800-322-0353

KENTUCKY
William P. Emrick, Executive Director
Office of Workers Claims
657 Chamberlin Avenue
Frankfort, KY 40601
(502) 564-5550 or 1-800-554-8601
(Contact: Patrick Roth)

LOUISIANA
Karen Winfrey, Asst. Secy./Dir.
Office of Workers' Compensation
1001 North 23rd Street
Baton Rouge, LA 70802-3338
(225) 342-7561 or 1-800-259-5154

MAINE
Paul R. Dionne, Exec. Director
Workers' Compensation Board
27 State House Station
Augusta, ME 04333-0027
(207) 287-3751 or 1-

MARYLAND
R. Karl Aumann, Chairman
Workers' Compensation Commission
10 East Baltimore Street
Baltimore, MD 21202-1641

Your Rights

Employment Guide

(Contact: Gwen Dugas)

800-400-6854
(Contact: Terrie McLaughlin)

(410) 864-5100 or 1-800-492-0479

MASSACHUSETTS
Paul Buckley,
Commissioner
Dept. of Industrial
Accidents
600 Washington Street,
7th Floor
Boston, MA 02111
(617) 727-4900 or 1-800-323-3249
(Contact: Edward Butts x483)

MICHIGAN
Jack A. Nolish,
Director
Department of
Energy, Labor &
Economic Growth
Workers'
Compensation
Agency
7150 Harris Drive
P. O. Box 30016
Lansing, MI 48909
(517) 322-1106 or 1-888-396-5041
(Contact: Sue Bickel)

MINNESOTA
Steve Sviggum,
Commissioner
Department of Labor
and Industry
Workers'
Compensation
Division
443 Lafayette Road
North
St. Paul, MN 55155-4319
(651) 284-5000 or 1-800-342-5354
(Contact: Brian Zaidman)

MISSISSIPPI
Liles Williams,
Chairman
Workers'
Compensation
Commission
1428 Lakeland Drive
P. O. Box 5300
Jackson, MS 39296-5300
(601) 987-4200 or 1-866-473-6922

MISSOURI
Jeff Buker, Director
Department of Labor
and Industrial
Relations
Division of Workers'
Compensation
3315 West Truman
Blvd., Room 131
P. O. Box 58
Jefferson City, MO 65102-0058
(573) 751-4231 or 1-800-775-2667

MONTANA
Jerry Keck,
Administrator
Employment
Relations Division
Department of Labor
and Industry
1805 Prospect
Avenue
P. O. Box 8011
Helena, MT 59604-8011
(406) 444-1555
(Contact: Diana

Carol D. Mitchell

NEBRASKA
Laureen K. Van Norman, Presiding Judge
Workers' Compensation Court
Capitol Building
P. O. Box 98908
Lincoln, NE 68509-8908
(402) 471-6468 or 1-800-599-5155

NEVADA
Roger Bremner, Administrator
Division of Industrial Relations
400 W. King Street, Suite 400
Carson City, NV 89703
(775) 684-7260
*Nancy Wong (for Profile Updates)

NEW HAMPSHIRE
Kathryn Barger, Director
Workers' Compensation Division
Department of Labor
95 Pleasant Street
Concord, NH 03301
(603) 271-3176 or 1-800-272-4353

NEW JERSEY
Peter Calderone, Dir./Chief Judge
Department of Labor and Workforce Development
Division of Workers' Compensation
P. O. Box 381
Trenton, NJ 08625-0381
(609) 292-2515

NEW MEXICO
Glenn R. Smith, Director
Workers' Compensation Admin.
2410 Centre Avenue, SE
P. O. Box 27198
Albuquerque, NM 87125-7198
(505) 841-6000 or 1-800-255-7965

NEW YORK
Zachary S. Weiss, Chair
Workers' Compensation Board
20 Park Street
Albany, NY 12207
(877) 632-4996
(Contact: Jon Sullivan)

NORTH CAROLINA
Pamela Young, Chair
Industrial Commission
4340 Mail Service Center
Raleigh, NC 27699-4340

NORTH DAKOTA
Charles Blunt, Exec. Dir.
Workforce Safety and Insurance
1600 East Century Avenue, Suite 1
Bismarck, ND

OHIO
Marsha P. Ryan, Administrator
Bureau of Workers' Compensation
30 West Spring Street
Columbus, OH 43215-2256
1-800-644-6292

Carol Denise Mitchell

Your Rights

Employment Guide

(919) 807-2500 or 1-800-688-8349

58503-0644
(701) 328-3800 or 1-800-777-5033

(Contact Norma J. Scott)

OKLAHOMA
Mary Black, Presid. Judge
Workers' Compensation Court
1915 North Stiles Avenue
Oklahoma City, OK 73105
(405) 522-8600 or 1-800-522-8210
(Contact: Tish Sommer)

OREGON
John Shilts, Administrator
Workers' Compensation Division
350 Winter Street, NE
P.O. Box 14480
Salem, OR 97309-0405
(503) 947-7810 or 1-800-452-0288

PENNSYLVANIA
John T. Kupchinsky, Director
Bureau of Workers' Compensation
Department of Labor and Industry
1171 So. Cameron Street, Rm. 324
Harrisburg, PA 17104-2501
(717) 783-5421 or 1-800-482-2383

PUERTO RICO
Basilio Rivera, Chairman
Industrial Commission
G.P.O. Box 364466
San Juan, PR 00936-4466
(787) 781-0545

RHODE ISLAND
E. Jean Severance, Associate Director
Department of Labor & Training
Division of Workers' Compensation
1511 Pontiac Ave.,Bld. 69,2nd Fl.
P. O. Box 20190
Cranston, RI 02920-0942
(401) 462-8100

SOUTH CAROLINA
Gary R. Thibault, Exec. Dir.
Workers' Compensation Commission
1612 Marion Street
P. O. Box 1715
Columbia, SC 29202-1715
(803) 737-5700
(Contact: Janet Godfrey Griggs)
(Second Injury –

Carol D. Mitchell

Mike Harris)

SOUTH DAKOTA
James Marsh,
Director
Department of Labor
Division of Labor &
Management
700 Governors Dr.,
Kneip Bldg.
Pierre, SD 57501-2291
(605) 773-3681

TENNESSEE
Sue Ann Head,
Administrator
Department of Labor
and Workforce
Development
Division of Workers'
Compensation
220 French Landing
Drive, 1st Floor, Side B
Nashville, TN 37243-1002
(615) 741-2395 or 1-800-332-2667
(Contact: Penny Shrum)

TEXAS
Albert Betts,
Commissioner
Department of
Insurance
Division of Workers'
Compensation
7551 Metro Center
Drive, Ste. 100
Austin, TX 78744-1609
(512) 804-4000 or 1-800-252-7031
(Contact: Laurie Crumpton)

UTAH
Joyce Sewell,
Director
Labor Commission
Division of Industrial
Accidents
160 East 300 South,
3rd Floor
P. O. Box 146610
Salt Lake City, UT 84114-6610
(801) 530-6800 or 1-800-530-5090

VERMONT
Steve Monahan,
Director
Workers' Compensation
Division
National Life Building,
Drawer 20
Montpelier, VT 05620-3401
(802) 828-2286 or 1-800-734-2286

VIRGINIA
Virginia R. Diamond,
Chairman
Workers'
Compensation
Commission
1000 DMV Drive
Richmond, VA 23220
(804) 367-8657 or 1-877-664-2566
(Contact: Sam Lupica)

VIRGIN ISLANDS
Idona Byron, Acting
Director
Department of Labor
Workers'
Compensation

WASHINGTON*
Robert Malooly,
Assistant Director
Department of Labor
and Industries
Insurance Services

WEST VIRGINIA
Jane L. Cline,
Insurance
Commissioner
Offices of the
Insurance

Carol Denise Mitchell

Your Rights

Employment Guide

Administration
3012 Vitraco Mall-
Golden Rock
St. Croix, VI 00820-4666
(809) 692-9390 or (809) 773-1994, Ext. 238

Division
7273 Linderson Way, SW
Tumwater, WA 98501-5414
(360) 902-5800 or 1-800-547-8367
*mailing address
P. O. Box 44100
Olympia, WA 98504-4100
(Contact: Laura Jenkins

Commission
1124 Smith Street
P.O. Box 50540
Charleston, WV 25301-0540
(304) 558-3386 or 1-888-879-9842

WISCONSIN
Francis Huntley-Cooper, Administrator
Department of Workforce Dev.
Workers' Compensation Division
201 East Washington Avenue
P. O. Box 7901
Madison, WI 53707-7901
(608) 266-1340
(Contact: Jean Culbert)

WYOMING
Gary W. Child, Director
Workers' Safety & Comp. Division
1510 East Pershing Boulevard
Cheyenne, WY 82002
(307) 777-7441
(Contact: Jamie Schaub)

Carol D. Mitchell

KEEP IT SIMPLE RESIGNATION LETTER

May 06, 20_____

To Whom It May Concern:

Per our discussion of May 5, 2---- I will resign my position as Manager of the *Hotel Maximum* on May 12, 2----.
Those being said, please accept this note as my official employment resignation.

Allow me to take a moment to say thank you to Gosling Investors, and Mr. Doe Winifred, for having allowed me this great five-year career opportunity.

Sincerely,

Jane Doe
29XXX Fruit Tree Way
Concord, CA 94520

Your Rights
Employment Guide

John Doe

Career Goal	Senior Electrical Engineer
	Washington, DC area.
Education	1999-2005 Graduate - Clark University
	Meridian, Idaho

SENIOR ELECTRICAL ENGINEERING

- B.S., Electrical Engineering, May 2----
- A.A.S., Electrical Engineering, December, 2---
- A.A.S., Computer Technology, May 2---

Awards Received	Dean's List, 1999-2005
	Electrical Engineering, 2----
	Honorary Society, 1998-2----
	Electronic Journeyman Award, 2----
	John F. Kennedy Scholarship, 1999-2----
Certificates	Electronic Mechanic Journeyman Certificate
	CPR, MTS and EMJ
Languages	English (fluent)
	Italian (working knowledge)
	Arabic (fluent)

Carol D. Mitchell

Chinese (fluent) (continued)

Profession 2000-2005 Bloomfield Trade School
Troy, Ohio
LEAD ELECTRICAL TECHNICIAN
- Worked as lead technician for the electrical engineering department
- Assisted instructors in the Engineering department during laboratory experiments

Volunteer Gold Medal of honor for fund raising/"Brave Men in Iraq"

Experience

Leadership Tiger Woods Youth Foundation Leader
activities Fundraiser for "Black Youths in Crisis"
Pitcher for "Vons" Red Team - 3 years

Your Rights

Employment Guide

CHAPTER 16
COVER LETTERS

Make your cover letter exciting. Spell everything right and try not to go over one page. Have the letter proofread by a reliable source. State in the letter that you plan to follow up with a phone call, but wait at least three days before inquiring about your candidacy for the job. Read the sample cover letter before for viable input into how your cover letter should be written.

Important Do's and Don'ts

Do: Spell check your cover letter

Do: Keep your letter short and succinct

Do: Have a reliable source proofread your letter

Do: Mail letter in a clean envelope free of coffee stains

Do not: Call the company prematurely to inquire about your application

Do not: Put personal anecdotes in your letter

Do not: Use pastel colored paper for your letter or resume

Do not: Talk about being fired in your letter

Do not: Call the company before three days to inquire about the job

Carol D. Mitchell

Jane Doe
619 XYZ Lane
Oakland, California 94607
510-452-XXXX
Cell (510) 484-XXXX
Janedoe2@eatyahoo.com

===

January 4, 2005
XYZ Company
P.O. Box XYZ
San Ramon, California 94583

RE: **Administrative Assistant Position**
       In Discovery Lab - Job Number 66678

Dear Department of Human Resources:

Attached, please find my resume for the *Administrative Assistant position* you advertised on your career-site today. I am seeking a versatile position chronicling the same core administrative duties that you outlined in your magnificent ad.

Upon review of my resume, you will see that attention to detail, and excellent organization are standard operations of which I have consistently demonstrated throughout my administrative career. As a manager, I worked well independently, as well as with others in a team setting. Overall, I truly believe that my professional skills match up perfect to what you are seeking in an administrative

Your Rights Employment Guide

assistant. Therefore, I submit to you my resume with the hope that I will meet with you soon to further discuss my professional abilities.

Here is thanking you advance for considering me for this great employment opportunity! I will follow-up with a telephone call soon to find out the status of this great career position.

Very truly yours,

Jane Doe
JD: cm

Enclosures: Resume (3 Pgs.)

Carol D. Mitchell

MORE GREAT RESUMES

In the pages ahead are some samples of great winning resumes that have really gotten people the job. When you create your resume, you are putting yourself in front of the employer to view your great experience and your masterful skills and talent. Therefore, keep the resume to one page. Use a simple layout that promotes professionalism. Look thoroughly into various job markets to select a company that you really want to work for. Be patient. Consider the totality of all your past work experiences to compile succinct notes that will allow you to choose the one company that is a right fit for you professionally. Know what you want in your *career objective* and say it. Treat your resume like a final term paper or short novel. Research, draft, cut and paste, until the words turn out saying the wonderful ideal true things about you that you want to exemplify to your new employer. Be prepared!

- Write down all of the things you are good at to organize your thoughts, checking off the things you like and the things you don't like in a workplace.
- Write down all of your skills. Don't leave the obscure things you did in your earlier work life out. For instance, if you worked *at Inland Meat Company* when you were twelve, write it down. Just because uncle Jeff did not pay you for that work experience for two summers, does not mean that you cannot

Your Rights
Employment Guide

get credit for the overall work experience and your great customer service and people skills.

- If you babysat your Aunt's or neighbor's kids for two summers, do not overlook the value of that work experience. You are patient, you are a problem solver and you are dependable and that adds up to experience. Use it or lose it.
- Remember that the person you are applying to for the job is human. If you are a member of a special charity, say so on your resume, and or in the job interview. Your new employer will most certainly appreciate the fact that you are a giving person who uses your free time to help others. Knowing who you are helps a company to consider you more seriously for the position.
- Review the sample resumes in this handbook to follow as a guide to properly prepare yourself to go out into the ever so growing competitive job market.

There will be over a million college graduates going into the job market this year. Do not let that intimidate you if you don't have a graduate degree. To get that special edge on others, apply for jobs when other's typically are not looking, like during the holiday season.

If you have worked your whole life supporting family, your work experience will have great value in the job market. A newly

Carol D. Mitchell

graduated college student still has to prove themselves in a new job market. If you want the job go after it. Convince the employer of your skills and ability to do the job. Have confidence in yourself. Follow all the rules, stay focused, pinpoint where you want to go and fulfil all of your work desires!

More tips:
- Make sure your home voicemail is free of slang and innuendos
- Use email addresses that are professional, not personal and crazy
- Leave the cell phone in the car glove compartment or at home during interviews
- Be serious about landing the job that you put so much effort in preparing for

Your Rights

Employment Guide

Great Resumes

ADMINISTRATIVE ASSISTANT PROFESSIONAL
HUMAN RESOURCES, OPERATIONS, & EXECUTIVE ADMINISTRATIVE SUPPORT

Knowledgeable, articulate business professional with over ten years of experience within security, healthcare administration, support administration, property management, writing, publishing, insurance, and legal environments. Demonstrated skill-set in organizational development, change management property management, and workforce initiatives designed to enhance efficiency, productivity, and profitability. Talent for managing complex projects involving multiple stakeholders to secure timely, quality-focused results. Maintain strong decision-making and problem-solving abilities, in addition to performance of data research analysis in development of high-impact programs.

Carol D. Mitchell

HIGHLIGHTS OF PROFESSIONAL EXPERIENCE

Administrative

- Successfully wrote, managed the application and publication of help guides, interview, and recruitment cycles, as part of career and workforce development efforts.
- Supported and managed varying fortune 500 entities as administrative support professional.
- Administrative support to: Doctors, Hospitals, Medical Clinics, Engineering firms.
- Responsible for performance of statistical, programmatic, and administrative analysis of application, recruitment, and rejection data.

Business

- Provision of a varied scope of consultative services to the Senior Management Nursing Team. Supported the Corporate Care Management Team Members and field-based Care Management Clinicians with the development and implementation of strategic initiatives to ensure the delivery of high quality healthcare services. Received training

Your Rights

Employment Guide

EMPLOYMENT HISTORY

2001-2005

Green-Tree Agency, *0512 Sansome Street, SF, CA 94104*

☐ **Administrative Assistant/Data Entry**

As an Administrative leader, I performed complicated online credit card entry into a perplexing alpha/numeric database. Administered, daily LAN backup and opened/sorted documents into batches of fifty, and then counted draft documents for the lead data entry clerk to proof and process for printing. Typed legal documents performing all duties as assigned by upper management and controlled the daily processing of all in/outgoing mail.

2000-2001

Plater Title Company, *0022 Battery Street, SF, CA 94111*

☐ **Proofreader**

Compared original documents against typed prelim reports, which consisted of the vesting legal description, taxes and exceptions by a title code book; made corrections for typist and prepared the prelim report(s) for the distribution clerk. Copied policies entered timed data into Access; performed all other duties as assigned by my supervisor.

Carol D. Mitchell

1995-2000

Third Brazilian Title, *10512 Spear Street, SF, CA 94103*

☐ **Alta Coordinator**

Contacted corporate IT daily for the computer system updates regarding the prelim reports status. Ordered search packages by county, received search packages by *U.S. mail*, *Federal Express* and fax. I assembled, distributed search packages to searchers by county; updated files for searchers, as well; pulled documents for the searchers by count and finished the process by performing all other administrative duties as requested by the supervisor.

1993-1995

Office Specialist, *3333 Sacramento Street, SF, CA 94102*

☐ **File Clerk Proofreader**

Filed title files into numerical order for title department and escrow; filed miscellaneous papers for escrow; also pulled files for recording desk, proofed *Limited Coverage Policies* for typist, entered data, assembled *LCP's* for mailing. Prepared envelopes for mailing by counties and for lenders by name and performed all other clerical duties as directed by my supervisor.

Your Rights

Employment Guide

SMART JOB OFFER LETTER

Mrs. Jane E. Doe
715 Greater Street - Apartment #16
San Francisco, CA 94110

May 16, 2005

Dear Ms. Doe:

This is to confirm our nuncupative conversation regarding our offer of new employment with New Starts Company (NSC). We are pleased that you have accepted the position of Assistant Manager, at the New Starts Company Headquarters, and we look forward to working with you here.

Your cash remuneration shall be $11.00 per hour, starting today. You will work (forty hours per week), full-time, Monday through Friday from 8:00 a.m. to 5:00 p.m. *(or as determined)*, with one hour off each day for lunch. You will report to the New Starts Academy, located at 3456 XXOO Drive, in the Presidio of San Francisco. Your immediate supervisor will be Mr. XYX.

You will be placed on probation for an introductory period of 180 days, starting your first day of work. After 90-days of full-time employment, you will be eligible for New Start's group health insurance and 401k plan with coverage starting the first day of the

Carol D. Mitchell

month following the 90-day probationary period.

Your employment is at-will. Therefore, during the course of your employment, you are free to leave New Start's Company at any time for any reason and NSC reserves a similar right. Thus, employment with the Company is not for a specified term and is therefore at the mutual consent of the employee and the Company.

On behalf of New Starts, welcome to the position of Assistant Manager. Please sign this letter below to acknowledge your acceptance of the offer.

— I accept this job offer

Your Rights Employment Guide

CHAPTER 17
The Improvisation Game

Do it right

You had a great resume and a great job interview and you got the job. Congratulations! Next, the employer ask you to do something that you don't know how to do. Before you ask your new employer how a task is done, find other ways to do it. Your friend Sara use to know how to do this task, but she has not done it in a long time and she said she forgot. What do I do? You need to know how to defend your present and future interest. Cut out the Microsoft "Cheat Sheet" in the previous chapter for quick reference. Tape it to your computer and learn shortcuts. Find the files that pertain to your specific task. Look into the file to see how it was done before and follow those directions to a tee. Never tell an employer that you simply can't or don't know how to do something that is material to your job. Companies are known to want things done in a consistent manner. Therefore, there is always tactile facts left behind by a previous worker that will help you learn how to effectively perform a task that you are not totally familiar with. If you are really stumped, visit the company web site or Intranet, or ask a knowledgeable co-worker for team player assistance. At the computer, type in the task. You will be surprised at how much help

Carol D. Mitchell

you will find. **Sample:** When you are not sure how to make a conference call or how to fill out an application right, review your guide for the professional and proper way to do it. Review the proper procedure on how to set up conference calls and be ahead of the pack. E-mail conference call participants ahead of time in case they will not be able to make the call. Tell them to email you back if they can't make a conference call. Copy their return message to all parties concerned ahead of the conference call time to alert them that a particular professional will not be able to participate in the call. Be a winner! Send a copy of your e-mail to your supervisor to let them know that you are an employee who is on top of your game!

NOTE:

Employment Applications No Longer need to be filed with State! One final feature of SB 1809 is the repeal of Labor Code section 431. This Labor Code previously required all employers to file a sample of their employment application(s) with the Division of Labor Standards Enforcement. No More!

Don't Play, do the Application thing right.:

You stayed up late last night at your partner's bungalow birthday party knowing that you have an important job interview tomorrow at 10:00 a.m. The application is complicated. You have been putting it off for 3 days, and now 6 hours before the interview, you don't feel like messing with it because you have a hangover.

You are a good person, but you do have a life. Just jot a few things

Your Rights
Employment Guide

down and hope the future employer has a crystal ball to see you for the dynamite cool person that you really are. **: Never** leave one line blank space in your job application no matter how great that you think you are. Review your application several times for correct spelling and date accuracy always.

If you don't have the energy to do it on your own, use your guide for the professional way to fill out a job application. Let the future employer know that you are energetic by turning in a well-completed list of your past work experience and education. Show the employer that you are earnest about getting a job with their great company. Show them that you do have the energy to complete your application with correct dates, superb spelling and attention to detail. **Remember this**: Your job application is the first impression to the employer of what kind of person that they are considering for this important job opening. *You are the right person for the job. So, act like it!!!*

Carol D. Mitchell

EXTENSIVE DETAILS ON WORKERS COMPENSATION
Division of Workers' Compensation fact sheet B
GLOSSARY OF WORKERS' COMPENSATION TERMS FOR INJURED WORKERS

Accepted claim: A claim in which the insurance company agrees your injury or illness is covered by workers' compensation. Even if your claim is accepted there may be delays or other problems. Also called admitted claim.

ACOEM: American College of Occupational and Environmental Medicine. Until the state Division of Workers' Compensation (DWC) adopts medical treatment guidelines, the guidelines published by ACOEM, called "Occupational Medicine Practice Guidelines," are the guidelines used in most cases to decide the type and amount of treatment you'll receive for a work injury or illness.

Agreed medical evaluator (AME): If you have an attorney, an AME is the doctor your attorney and the insurance company agree on to conduct the medical examination that will help resolve your dispute. If you don't have an attorney, you will use a qualified medical evaluator (QME). See QME.

Alternative work: A new job with your former employer. If your doctor says you will not be able to return to your job at the time of injury, your employer is encouraged to offer you alternative work instead of supplemental job displacement benefits or vocational rehabilitation benefits. The alternative work must meet your work

Your Rights
Employment Guide

restrictions, last at least 12 months, pay at least 85 percent of the wages and benefits you were paid at the time you were injured, and be within a reasonable commuting distance of where you lived at the time of injury.

American Medical Association (AMA): A national physician's group. The AMA publishes a set of guidelines called "Guides to the Evaluation of Permanent Impairment." If your permanent disability is rated under the 2005 rating schedule, the doctor is required to determine your level of impairment using the AMA's guides.

Americans with Disabilities Act (ADA): A federal law that prohibits discrimination against people with disabilities. If you believe you've been discriminated against at work because you're disabled and want information on your rights under the ADA, contact a U.S. Equal Employment Opportunity Commission office. For the EEOC office in your area, call 1-800-669-4000 or 1-800-669-6820 (TTY).

AOE/COE (Arising out of and occurring in the course of employment): Your injury must be caused by and happen on the job.

Applicant: The party -- usually you -- that opens a case at the local Workers' Compensation Appeals Board (WCAB) office by filing an application for adjudication of claim.

Carol D. Mitchell

Appeals board: A group of seven commissioners appointed by the governor to review and reconsider decisions of workers' compensation administrative law judges. Also called the Reconsideration Unit. See Workers' Compensation Appeals Board.

Applicants' attorney: A lawyer that can represent you in your workers' compensation case. Applicant refers to you, the injured worker.

Application for adjudication of claim (application or app): A form you file to open a case at the local Workers' Compensation Appeals Board (WCAB) office if you have a disagreement with the insurance company about your claim.

Apportionment: A way of figuring out how much of your permanent disability is due to your work injury and how much is due to other disabilities.

Audit Unit: A unit within the DWC that receives complaints against claims administrators. These complaints may lead to investigations of the way the company handles claims.

Benefit notice: A required letter or form sent to you by the insurance company to inform you of benefits you may be entitled to receive. Also called notice.

Cal/OSHA: A unit within the state Division of Occupational Safety and Health (DOSH). Cal/OSHA inspects workplaces and enforces laws to protect the health and safety of workers in California.

California Labor Code section 132a: A workers' compensation law that prohibits discrimination against you because you filed a

Your Rights
Employment Guide

workers' compensation claim, and against co-workers who might testify in your case.

Carve-out: Carve-out programs allow employers and unions to create their own alternatives for workers' compensation benefit delivery and dispute resolution under a collective bargaining agreement.

Claim form: The form used to report a work injury or illness to your employer.

Claims adjuster: See claims administrator.

Claims administrator: The term for insurance companies and others that handle your workers' compensation claim. Most claims administrators work for insurance companies or third party administrators handling claims for employers. Some claims administrators work directly for large employers that handle their own claims. Also called claims examiner or claims adjuster.

Claims examiner: See claims administrator.

Commission on Health and Safety and Workers' Compensation (CHSWC): A state-appointed body that conducts studies and makes recommendations to improve the California workers' compensation and workplace health and safety systems.

Commutation: An order by a workers' compensation judge for a lump sum payment of part or all of your permanent disability award.

Carol D. Mitchell

Compromise and release (C&R): A type of settlement in which you receive a lump sum payment and become responsible for paying for your future medical care. A settlement like this must be approved by a workers' compensation judge.

Cumulative injury (CT): An injury that was caused by repeated events or repeated exposures at work. For example, hurting your wrist doing the same motion over and over or losing your hearing because of constant loud noise.

Date of injury: When you got hurt or ill. If your injury was caused by one event, the date it happened is the date of injury. If the injury or illness was caused by repeated exposures (a cumulative injury), the date of injury is the date you knew or should have known the injury was caused by work.

Death benefits: Benefits paid to surviving dependents when a work injury or illness results in death.

Declaration of readiness (DOR or DR): A form used to request a hearing before a workers' compensation judge when you're ready to resolve a dispute.

Defendant: The party — usually your employer or its insurance company -- opposing you in a dispute over benefits or services.

Delay letter: A letter sent to you by the insurance company that explains why payments are delayed. The letter also tells you what information is needed before payments will be sent and when a decision will be made about the payments.

Denied claim: A claim in which the insurance company believes

Your Rights

Employment Guide

your injury or illness is not covered by workers' compensation and has notified you of the decision.

Description of employee's job duties (RU-91): A form filled out jointly by you and the insurance company that helps your treating physician decide whether you will be able to return to your normal job and working conditions.

Determination and order (D&O): A decision by the DWC Rehabilitation Unit on a vocational rehabilitation dispute.

Disability: A physical or mental impairment that limits your life activities. A condition that makes engaging in physical, social and work activities difficult.

Carol D. Mitchell

Disability Evaluation Unit (DEU): A unit within the DWC that calculates the percent of permanent disability based on medical reports. See disability rater.

Disability management: A process to prevent disability from occurring or to intervene early, following the start of a disability, to encourage and support continued employment. This is done early in the recovery process in severe injury cases such as spinal injuries. Usually a rehabilitation nurse is involved with you and your treating doctor and the progress of your medical treatment is reported to the insurance company.

Disability rater: An employee of the DWC Disability Evaluation Unit who rates your permanent disability after reviewing a medical report or a medical-legal report describing your condition.

Disability rating: See permanent disability rating.

Discrimination claim (Labor Code132a): A petition filed if your employer has fired or otherwise discriminated against you for filing a workers' compensation claim.

Dispute: A disagreement about your right to payments, services or other benefits.

Division of Workers' Compensation (DWC): A division within the state Department of Industrial Relations (DIR). The DWC administers workers' compensation laws, resolves disputes over workers' compensation benefits and provides information and assistance to injured workers and others about the workers' compensation system.

Employee: A person whose work activities are under the control

Your Rights
Employment Guide

of an individual or entity. The term employee includes undocumented workers and minors.

Employer: The person or entity with control over your work activities.

Ergonomics: The study of how to improve the fit between the physical demands of the workplace and the employees who perform the work. That means considering the variability in human capabilities when selecting, designing or modifying equipment, tools, work tasks and the work environment.

Essential functions: Duties considered crucial to the job you want or have. When being considered for alternative work, you must have both the physical and mental qualifications to fulfill the job's essential functions.

Fair Employment and Housing Act (FEHA): A state law that prohibits discrimination against people with disabilities. If you believe you've been discriminated against at work because you're disabled and want more information on your rights under the FEHA, contact the state Department of Fair Employment and Housing at 1-800-884-1684. In some cases, the FEHA provides more protection than the federal Americans with Disabilities Act (ADA).

Family and Medical Leave Act (FMLA): A federal law that provides certain employees with serious health problems or who

Carol D. Mitchell

need to care for a child or other family member with up to 12 weeks of unpaid, job-protected leave per year. It also requires that group health benefits be maintained during the leave. For more information, contact the U.S. Department of Labor at 1-866-4-USA-DOL.

Prepared by
the Office of the Assistant Secretary for Policy

Updated: February 2008

This Guide describes the statutes and regulations administered by the U.S. Department of Labor (DOL) that affect businesses and workers. The Guide is designed mainly for those needing "hands-on" information to develop wage, benefit, safety and health, and nondiscrimination policies for businesses in general industry.

Note: The federal minimum wage for covered, nonexempt employees increased to $5.85 per hour effective July 24, 2007; $6.55 per hour effective July 24, 2008; and $7.25 per hour effective July 24, 2009. Most changes are related to the minimum wage increase, although small revisions were also made in Chapters B and D.

Also, the Family and Medical Leave Act of 1993 (FMLA) was amended on January 28, 2008. Section 585 of the National Defense Authorization Act for FY 2008 amends the FMLA to permit a "spouse, son, daughter, parent, or next of kin" to take up to 26 workweeks of leave to care for a "member of the Armed Forces, including a member of the National Guard or Reserves, who is

Your Rights
Employment Guide

undergoing medical treatment, recuperation, or therapy, is otherwise in outpatient status, or is otherwise on the temporary disability retired list, for a serious injury or illness." Additional information is available on the Wage and Hour Division's Web site.

The February 2008 errata sheet lists all the changes that have been made to various pages of the Employment Law Guide.

Filing: Sending or delivering a document to an employer or a government agency as part of a legal process. The date of filing is the date the document is received.

Final order: Any order, decision or award made by a workers' compensation judge that has not been appealed in a timely way.

Findings & award (F&A): A written decision by a workers' compensation administrative law judge about your case, including payments and future care that must be provided to you. The F&A becomes a final order unless appealed.

Fraud: Any knowingly false or fraudulent statement for the purpose of obtaining or denying workers' compensation benefits. The penalties for committing fraud are fines up to $150,000 and/or imprisonment for up to five years.

Future medical: On-going right to medical treatment for a work-related injury.

Health care organization (HCO): An organization certified by

Carol D. Mitchell

the Department of Industrial Relations to provide managed medical care within the workers' compensation system.

Hearings: Legal proceedings in which a workers' compensation judge discusses the issues in a case or receives information in order to make a decision about a dispute or a proposed settlement.

In pro per: An injured worker not represented by an attorney.

Independent contractor: There is no set definition of this term. Labor law enforcement agencies and the courts look at several factors when deciding if someone is an employee or an independent contractor. Some employers misclassify employees as an independent contractor to avoid workers' compensation and other payroll responsibilities. Just because an employer says you are an independent contractor and doesn't need to cover you under a workers' compensation policy doesn't make it true. A true independent contractor has control over how their work is done. You probably are not an independent contractor when the person paying you:

- Controls the details or manner of your work
- Has the right to terminate you
- Pays you an hourly wage or salary
- Makes deductions for unemployment or Social Security
- Supplies materials or tools
- Requires you to work specific days or hours

Your Rights
Employment Guide

Industrial Medical Council (IMC): No longer in existence. See Medical Unit.

Information & Assistance Unit (I&A): A unit within DWC that provides information to all parties in workers' compensation claims and informally resolves disputes.

Information & Assistance (I&A) officer: A DWC employee who answers questions, assists injured workers, provides written materials, conducts informational workshops and holds meetings to informally resolve problems with claims.

Injury and illness prevention program (IIPP): A health and safety program employers are required to develop and implement. This program is enforced by Cal/OSHA.

Impairment rating: A percentage estimate of how much normal use of your injured body parts you've lost. Impairment ratings are determined based on guidelines published by the American Medical Association (AMA). An impairment rating is used to calculate your permanent disability rating but is different from your permanent disability rating.

Judge: See workers' compensation administrative law judge.

Lien: A right or claim for payment against a workers' compensation case. A lien claimant, such as a medical provider, can file a form with the local Workers' Compensation Appeals

Board to request payment of money owed in a workers' compensation case.

Mandatory settlement conference (MSC): A required conference to discuss settlement prior to a trial.

Maximal medical improvement (MMI): Your condition is well stabilized and unlikely to change substantially in the next year, with or without medical treatment. Once you reach MMI, a doctor can assess how much, if any, permanent disability resulted from your work injury.

Mediation conference: A voluntary conference held before an I&A officer to resolve a dispute if you are not represented by an attorney.

Medical care: See medical treatment.

Medical-legal report: A report written by a doctor that describes your medical condition. These reports are written to help clarify disputed medical issues.

Medical provider network (MPN): An entity or group of health care providers set up by an insurer or self-insured employer and approved by DWC's administrative director to treat workers injured on the job.

Medical treatment: Treatment reasonably required curing or relieving the effects of a work-related injury or illness. Also called medical care.

Medical Unit: A unit within the DWC that oversees medical provider networks (MPNs), independent medical review (IMR)

Your Rights
Employment Guide

physicians, health care organizations (HCOs), qualified medical evaluators (QMEs), panel QMEs, utilization review (UR) plans, and spinal surgery second opinion physicians. Formerly called the Industrial Medical Council (IMC).

Modified work: Your old job, with some changes that allow you do to it. If your doctor says you will not be able to return to your job at the time of injury, your employer is encouraged to offer you modified work instead of supplemental job displacement benefits or vocational rehabilitation benefits.

Nontransferable voucher: A document you get from the insurance company that must be completed by both you and the insurance company. This is the document used to provide payment for education under the supplemental job displacement benefit program.

Notice: See benefit notice.

Objective factors: Measurements, direct observations and test results a treating physician, QME or an AME says contribute to your permanent disability.

Off calendar (OTOC): A WCAB case in which there is no pending action.

Offer of modified or alternative work form (RU-94): A form you get from the insurance company if: you were injured before 2004 and; your treating physician says you probably will never

Carol D. Mitchell

return to your job or one like it and; your employer is offering modified or alternative work instead of vocational rehabilitation benefits.

Offer of modified or alternative work (DWC form #AD 10133.53): A form you get from the insurance company if: you were injured in 2004 or later and; your treating physician reports you have a permanent disability and; your employer is offering modified or alternative work instead of a supplemental job displacement benefit. This form also explains how your permanent disability payments may be lowered by 15 percent because your employer is returning you to work.

Panel qualified medical evaluator (QME): A list of three independent qualified medical evaluators (QMEs) issued by the DWC Medical Unit. You select any one of the three doctors for your evaluation. If you have an attorney, other rules apply.

Party: Normally this includes the insurance company, your employer, attorneys and any other person with an interest in your claim (doctors or hospitals that have not been paid).

Permanent and stationary (P&S): Your medical condition has reached maximum medical improvement. Once you are P&S, a doctor can assess how much, if any, permanent disability resulted from your work injury. If your disability is rated under the 2005 schedule you will see the term maximal medical improvement (MMI) used in place of P&S. See also P&S report.

Permanent disability (PD): Any lasting disability that results in a reduced earning capacity after maximum medical improvement is

Your Rights
Employment Guide

reached.

Permanent disability rating (PDR): A percentage that estimates how much a job injury permanently limits the kinds of work you can do. It is based on your medical condition, date of injury, age when injured, occupation when injured, how much of the disability is caused by your job, and your diminished future earning capacity. It determines the number of weeks you are entitled to permanent disability benefits.

Permanent disability rating schedule (PDRS): A DWC publication containing detailed information used to rate permanent disabilities. One of three schedules will be used to rate your disability, depending on when you were injured.

Permanent disability (PD) benefits: Payments you receive when your work injury permanently limits the kinds of work you can do or your ability to earn a living.

Permanent disability advance (PDA): A *voluntary* lump sum payment of permanent disability you are due in the future.

Permanent disability payments: A mandatory bi-weekly payment based on the undisputed portion of permanent disability received before and/or after an award is issued.

Permanent partial disability award: A final award of permanent partial disability made by a workers' compensation judge or the Workers' Compensation Appeals Board.

Carol D. Mitchell

Permanent partial disability (PPD) benefits: Payments you receive when your work injury partially limits the kinds of work you can do or your ability to earn a living.

Permanent total disability (PTD) benefits: Payments you receive when you are considered permanently unable to earn a living.

Penalty: An amount of money you receive because something wasn't done correctly in your claim. Paid by your employer or the insurance company, the penalty amount can be an automatic 10 percent for a delay in one payment to you, or a 25 percent penalty -- up to $10,000 -- for an unreasonable delay.

Personal physician: A doctor licensed in California with an M.D. degree (medical doctor) or a D.O. degree (osteopath), who has treated you in the past and has your medical records.

Petition for reconsideration (Recon): A legal process to appeal a decision issued by a workers' compensation judge. Heard by the Workers' Compensation Appeals Board Reconsideration Unit, a seven-member, judicial body appointed by the governor and confirmed by the Senate.

Physician: A medical doctor, an osteopath, a psychologist, an acupuncturist, an optometrist, a dentist, a podiatrist or a chiropractor licensed in California. The definition of personal physician is more limited. See personal physician.

Pre-designated physician: A physician that can treat your work injury if you advised your employer in writing prior to your work injury or illness and certain conditions are met. See pre-designation.

Your Rights
Employment Guide

Pre-designation: The process you use to tell your employer you want your personal physician to treat you for a work injury. You can pre-designate your personal doctor of medicine (M.D.) or doctor of osteopathy (D.O.) if: your employer offers group health coverage; the doctor has treated you in the past and has your medical records; prior to the injury your doctor agreed to treat you for work injuries or illnesses and; prior to the injury you provided your employer the following in writing:

(1) Notice that you want your personal doctor to treat you for a work-related injury or illness and

(2) Your personal doctor's name and business address.

Primary treating physician (PTP): The doctor having overall responsibility for treatment of your work injury or illness. This physician writes medical reports that may affect your benefits. Also called treating physician or treating doctor.

Proof of service: A form used to show that documents have been sent to specific parties.

P&S report: A medical report written by a treating physician that describes your medical condition when it has stabilized. See also permanent and stationary.

Qualified injured worker (QIW): Entitled to vocational rehabilitation benefits. This benefit applies only if you were injured before Jan. 1, 2004.

Carol D. Mitchell

Qualified medical evaluator (QME): An independent physician certified by the DWC Medical Unit to perform medical evaluations.

Qualified rehabilitation representative (QRR): A person trained and able to evaluate, counsel, and place disabled workers in new jobs. Also called rehabilitation counselor.

Rating: See permanent disability rating.

Reconsideration: See petition for reconsideration.

Reconsideration Unit: See appeals board.

Reconsideration of a summary rating: A process used when you don't have an attorney and you think mistakes were made in your permanent disability rating.

Regular work: Your old job, paying the same wages and benefits as paid at the time of an injury and located within a reasonable commuting distance of where you lived at the time of your injury.

Rehabilitation consultant: A DWC employee who oversees vocational rehabilitation procedures, makes decisions about vocational rehabilitation benefits and helps resolve disputes.

Rehabilitation counselor: See qualified rehabilitation representative (QRR).

Rehabilitation Unit: A unit within DWC that resolves vocational rehabilitation disputes, approves potential settlements of vocational rehabilitation services, and reviews and approves vocational rehabilitation plans for injuries that happened before Jan. 1, 2004.

Restrictions: See work restrictions.

Your Rights Employment Guide

Schedule for rating permanent disabilities: See permanent disability rating schedule.

Settlement: An agreement between you and the insurance company about your workers' compensation payments and future medical care. Settlements must be reviewed by a workers' compensation judge to make sure they are adequate.

Serious and willful misconduct (S&W): A petition filed if your injury is caused by the serious and willful misconduct of your employer.

Social Security disability benefits: Long-term financial assistance for totally disabled persons. These benefits come from the U.S. Social Security Administration. They are reduced by workers' compensation payments you receive.

Specific injury: An injury caused by one event at work. Examples: hurting your back in a fall, getting burned by a chemical splashed on your skin, getting hurt in a car accident while making deliveries.

State average weekly wage: The average weekly wage paid in the previous year to employees in California covered by unemployment insurance, as reported by the U.S. Department of Labor. Effective 2006, temporary disability benefit increases are tied to this index.

Carol D. Mitchell

State disability insurance (SDI): A partial wage-replacement insurance plan paid out to California workers by the state Employment Development Department (EDD). SDI provides short-term benefits to eligible workers who suffer a loss of wages when they are unable to work due to a non-work-related illness or injury, or a medically disabling condition from pregnancy or childbirth. Workers with job injuries may apply for SDI when workers' compensation payments are delayed or denied. Call 1-800-480-3287 for more information on SDI.

Stipulated rating: Formal agreement on your permanent disability rating. Must be approved by a workers' compensation judge.

Stipulation with award: A settlement of a case where the parties agree on the terms of an award. This is the document the judge signs to make the award final.

Stipulations with request for award (Stips): A settlement in which the parties agree on the terms of an award. It may include future medical treatment. Payment takes place over time. This document is provided to the judge for final review.

Subjective factors: The amount of pain and other symptoms described by an injured worker that a doctor reports as contributing to a worker's permanent disability. Subjective factors are given very little weight under the 2005 rating schedule as the schedule relies mainly on objective measurements.

Subpoena: A document that requires a witness to appear at a

Your Rights Employment Guide

hearing.

Subpoena Duces Tecum (SDT): A document that requires records be sent to the requester.

Summary rating: The percentage of permanent disability calculated by the DWC Disability Evaluation Unit.

Summary rating reconsideration: A procedure used if you object to the summary rating issued by the DWC Disability Evaluation Unit.

Supplemental job displacement benefit (SJDB): A workers' compensation benefit. If you were injured in 2004 or later, and have a permanent partial disability that prevents you from doing your old job, and your employer does not offer other work, you qualify for this benefit. It is in the form of a voucher that promises to help pay for educational retraining or skill enhancement, or both, at state-approved or state-accredited schools. Also called voucher.

Temporary disability (TD or TTD): Payments you get if you lose wages because your injury prevents you from doing your usual job while recovering.

Temporary partial disability (TPD) benefits: Payments you get if you can do some work while recovering, but you earn less than before the injury.

Temporary total disability (TTD) benefits: Payments you get if

Carol D. Mitchell

you cannot work at all while recovering.

Transportation expenses: A benefit to cover your out-of-pocket expenses for mileage, parking and toll fees related to a claim. Usually a reimbursement.

Treating doctor: See primary treating physician.

Treating physician: See primary treating physician.

Uninsured Employers Fund (UEF): A fund, run by the DWC, through which your benefits can be paid if your employer is illegally uninsured for workers' compensation.

Utilization review (UR): The process used by insurance companies to decide whether to authorize and pay for treatment recommended by your treating physician or another doctor.

Vocational & return to work counselor (VRTWC): If you have a permanent disability, this is the person or entity that helps you develop a return to work strategy. They evaluate you, provide counseling and help you get ready to work. A VRTWC must have at least an undergraduate degree in any field and three or more years of full time experience.

Vocational rehabilitation (VR): A workers' compensation benefit. If you were injured before 2004 and are permanently unable to do your usual job, and your employer does not offer other work, you qualify for this benefit. It includes job placement counseling to help you find another job. It may also include retraining and a vocational rehabilitation maintenance allowance.

Your Rights
Employment Guide

Vocational rehabilitation maintenance allowance (VRMA): Payments to help you with living expenses while participating in vocational rehabilitation. See vocational rehabilitation.

Voucher: See supplemental job displacement benefit and nontransferable voucher.

Wage loss (temporary partial disability): See temporary partial disability benefits.

Workers' Compensation Appeals Board (WCAB): Consists of 24 local offices throughout the state where disagreements over workers' compensation benefits are initially heard by workers' compensation judges. The WCAB Reconsideration Unit in San Francisco is a seven-member, judicial body appointed by the governor and confirmed by the Senate that hears appeals of decisions issued by local workers' compensation judges.

Workers' Compensation Insurance Rating Bureau (WCIRB): An agent of the state Department of Insurance and funded by the insurance industry, this private entity provides statistical and rating information for workers' compensation insurance and employer's liability insurance, and collects and tabulates information to develop pure premium rates.

Work restrictions: A doctor's description of the work you can and cannot do. Work restrictions help protect you from

Carol D. Mitchell

further injury.

Workers' compensation administrative law judge: A DWC employee who makes decisions about workers' compensation disputes and approves settlements. Judges hold hearings at local Workers' Compensation Appeals Board (WCAB) offices, and their decisions may be reviewed and reconsidered by the Reconsideration Unit of the WCAB. Also called workers' compensation judge.

Workers' compensation judge: See workers' compensation administrative law judge.

The information contained in this fact sheet is general in nature and is not intended as a substitute for legal advice. Changes in the law or the specific facts of your case may result in legal interpretations different than those presented here.

DWC fact sheet B
Rev. 7/05

Your Rights Employment Guide

SMART TIP!

Smart Classification

In order to move on in your career and be earnest about your future, you need to know what functions, duties and skills are expected of you in your new job. Please review the standard job classification below to make sure you are ready for your ideal job. Write down all of your work experience. Next, make a checklist of your strong skill set before creating your winning resume. Your efforts may reveal that you are qualified indeed for many different hot jobs!

Carol D. Mitchell

Chapter 18
Temporary Rights

As a Temporary, Contingent or Contract worker, you have the same rights as permanent employees to not be discriminated against in the American workplace. Neither the agency nor the Contract Company where you work can discriminate against you because of your race, sex, religion, color, national origin, age or disability. Both the agency you work for and the company that they send you to share responsibility for making sure that you are not exposed to illegal discrimination

In spite of laws that protect all workers, many temporary workers face illegal discrimination in the workplace. It is important for temporary workers to know their rights and demand the respect that they deserve on the job.

Am I a Temporary Worker

You are a temporary employee if you are employed by a temporary employment agency and they place you at another company's work place. In this case, both the agency staff and the management staff may supervise you where they send you to work. In the scheme of things, you are contracted out to another company. You can tell by whose being in charge, the agency or the company where you

Your Rights
Employment Guide

work who is the boss. As a temporary worker, it is safe to assume that both the agency and the company that you are sent to are both your bosses. In order to gauge further, who is ultimately responsible for you as a temporary worker, ascertain who is supplying the fundamental tools, materials or equipment that you are going to work with. Are you working in a private business for yourself or not? How are you paid? Do you receive benefits? Since there may be many other factors that can render you to be a temporary worker, call the ERA or other organizations to find out more information about your temporary employment status.

<u>Remember</u>: If you are discriminated against as a temporary worker, the responsibility may fall on both the agency that employs you and the company they sent you to. The agency should stop the discrimination. In addition, the company they send you to may be responsible if they are supervising your work and control over you during your interim assignment. Ask yourself if the agency and the company both share or split duties.

<u>Remember</u>: If things go wrong on your assignment, you have the right to go through your agency's complaint process. Write down the complaint and complain to both companies. File a charge against the temporary agency and

Carol D. Mitchell

the place where they sent you to work with a state or federal agency.

Follow the same rules that the regular fully employed worker does when filing your state or federal claim. Talk with an employment lawyer to acquire more information on exercising your full rights. People who implement these laws as a working professional have a better understanding of how you can legally pursue your rights. Like the regular full-time employee, remember to document your case, and keep copious records and keep a paper trail of work events.

Always use the company's complaint or grievance process to resolve any problems you may experience on the job. You can call ERA"S advice and counseling line at 1-800-839-4ERA for more information regarding your temporary employee rights.

<u>Great Employee (help) resources to call below NOTE:</u> <u>*Check the yellow pages if numbers and or locations change.*</u>

Your Rights
Employment Guide

California Equal Employment **Opportunity Commission (EEOC)**
901 Market Street - Suite #500
San Francisco, CA 94103
415-356-5100

California Department of Fair **Employment and Housing (DFEH)**
30 Van Ness Ave., Suite #3000
San Francisco, CA 94102
(800) 884-1684
Employment Law Center
Workers' Rights Clinics

East Bay, South Bay, San Francisco
(415) 864-8208
La Raza Centro Legal
474 Valencia St., Suite #295
San Francisco, CA 94103
(415) 575-3500

Chinese for Affirmative Action
17 Walter U. Lum Place
San Francisco, CA 94108

Carol D. Mitchell

(415) 274-6750

(Chinese Services Available - Cantonese and Mandarin)

NOW Legal Defense and Education **Fund**

99 Hudson St., 12th Floor

New York, NY 10013

(212) 925-6635

9 to 5 National Association of Working Women

231 West Wisconsin Avenue - Suite #900

Milwaukee, WI 53203

(800) 522-0925

Your Rights
Employment Guide

The rule of most agencies is, *"never walk off of your temporary assignment." Therefore* as you are reading, take heed to how Jean handled her unimaginable temporary work experience.

Jean was a middle-aged temporary worker who was sent to what is perhaps arguably, the worst temporary assignment ever.

It was the bad hair age of the 90's' and the innovative times of the dot.com computer wars. As a temporary worker it was hard to predict where Jean, at age 41 might end up on any given day. On a brisk spring morning, Jean was on her way to one of the most beautiful offices on the Embarcadero. San Francisco had bestowed her with great optimism and its awesome wonder. Jean thought she had entered heaven. Off the smooth escalator ride, Jean floated into the fine red and black checkerboard, plush carpeted area of the cool offices of the most elite-consulting firm in the city. Inside the plush sanctuary, Jean met beautiful account reps and professional people who were sat aside from the rest of the world. Ten minutes into the office, a lovely Paris Hilton type greeted Jean kindly. Then, with her porcelain left hand she swept Jean into the pine smelling, private confines of the companies most spectacular, well-polished, silver and lime conference room.

"Have a seat," she told Jean. Jean sat on a bright red chair and Heather sat next to her in a blue one. At the long green and black

Carol D. Mitchell

marble conference room table, Heather introduced herself to be a "Senior Account Representative." From a setting center the conference room table, she offered Jean a cup of freshly brewed coffee served in an expensive black, stone-brine coffee mug bearing the Company's impressive red cobra logo.

"Thanks!" said Jean, as she caressed the hot cup with both hands.

"You're welcome Jean. I hope you don't get hot in that nice suit you are wearing," she said, referring to the expensive, black Jones of New York attire Jean had on. After sipping great coffee and giggling at Heather's cordial niceties, Jean accepted her black office key from Heather. Then the pretty "Senior Account Representative," led her temporary worker to the 2x4 confines of a narrow closet, below the basement of the conference room.

"This is the assignment she said. I am told by the agency that you are not claustrophobic. They said you mentioned on your application that you are able to work anywhere. So we want you to look out this peep-hole and simply write down everything you see next door." She said.

On the part of Jean, kindness spun into brutal aloofness, as it was important to Jean to hold back her shock of her assignment location. The dark closet was a 2x4 office, with no windows. The large peephole that had been savagely drilled into the next door neighbors wall was frightening. When Heather left, Jean cried. Soon Heather came back.

Your Rights
Employment Guide

"Oh! I forgot to tell you Jean. Do not let the competition see or hear you. We just want you to watch what comes up on Mr. Neighbor's computer screens and stuff like that." She whispered. Jean heard Heather's annoying voice, but she could not see her, because, there was no room for two people in the closet. Therefore, Heather voiced her instructions to Jean from the enclave of the shadowy hallway.

"Use the number two pencil with the yellow legal paper pad to write down everything you see. I am sorry it is darker down here than I care to admit. Jean, I know that you are an intelligent woman, so you know why we simply cannot use these lights. You have 30-minutes for lunch. Lock up. You will have no relief." She stated. When Heather left the deserted work area, Jean squat down onto a prickly wood plank floor to get reception on her cell telephone to call the agency. The call was dropped endlessly, before she got through. When she finally reached her agent, to verify the duties of the strange

assignment, the agent listened quietly. Next, she assured Jean she could stick it out. "After all," she said, "where else are you going to find $38.00 an hour for surveying a peephole in an 8 hour day?" She asked her.

Later, Jean checked her voicemail to see if a real job had called. There were no messages. Coming up off the floor, she hit her head

Carol D. Mitchell

on a rough piece of 2x4 plywood that was her desk. Then she watched the neighbor play Solitaire from a red computer screen while his office mates spent the day surfing the web for mostly E-news sites. Soon Jean's neck got stiff. Later, her head fell into her chest so hard that she nearly knocked herself unconscious. The LAN system on top her head began screeching loudly in her ears. Then flying white dust mites chewed tiny holes into Jean's suit, creating a freeway to her needled skin. Suddenly, she began to itch all over. Next, a gray, powder like substance, drifted into her nose. She sneezed loud enough for the competition to turn their heads towards the secret peephole to see where the noise was coming from. Suddenly, this cat and mouse temporary assignment took on the feeling to Jean of being in a dark coal mine. Three hours into the assignment Jean's right eye was bruised from looking through the jagged peephole. Her finest suit was drenched with sweat that formed puddles into her lap. Jean had spent so much time trying to adjust to her unbearable prison, that she had not written a word. The continual screeches from the LAN above left her spinning like a top until she was completely, unable to concentrate. As she anticipated an end to this hell, Jean, the well-intended worker, simply allowed her body to slowly retreat into an abrupt, coma like sleep.

"Wake up!" Heather shouted. "You are the third temp to come here and fall asleep on this project. What is so hard about sitting in a room and taking notes?" She asked her. Next, she snatched the wet pad out of the clutches of Jean's numb fingers.

Your Rights
Employment Guide

You have not recorded a thing!" She shouted, dropping the yellow legal pad on the floor. Soon Jean was jolted out of her surprise sleep, to find that she was dehydrated. In the meantime, Heather continued to rage over the missing notes.

It was the first time in Jean's work career that she slept on the job from being mistreated and exhausted. However, she deferred defending herself. She would save it for the judge because she knew that she was going to be fired. When Heather kicked her out of the office that evening, the next day, the agency she gave five years of her life to fired her. To Jean, it was the best thing they could have done for her. After that experience, she was just grateful to be alive!

When Jean appealed the company's denial of her Unemployment Insurance benefits and the firing, the administrative law judge, for the State of California Unemployment Appeals Board, sided with the temporary worker. Therefore, Jean was given all of her unemployment benefits. At the appeal hearing, the smart judge tore into the agency for not moving Jean after her call to them from the condemnable work situation.

Good for Jean! She knew her rights and she accepted her fate without drama or fanfare. She called her agency in an appropriate and timely manner.

Carol D. Mitchell

Chapter 19

The Five Star ◊ Superior You

It is not a bad ideal to prepare yourself fully for your big interview day. Rehearse your interview the night before with a friend to ensure that all of your responses to questions are accurate, and in line with the question that is being asked. Do not donate information that is not being asked of you. Play it safe. Use common sense to answer general interview questions. Bring your manners. After the interviewer questions you, politely say, "thank you." Do not babble on and on in your interview. Do not leave the impression that you are crazy or unstable and that if they hire you you might be a potential liability to the company. Stay in the middle and in job interviews always be professional. Keep in mind that you are being rated on everything from how you look to what you say, and in some cases what you don't say. After the interview, and when you get the job, stay away from office clicks. Do not gossip. Stay neutral for at least ninety days into your new job.

Additionally, do your homework. Thoroughly research the company on the Web. Be prepared to know who leads as CEO, president, and particularly learn what their special

Your Rights
Employment Guide

accomplishments and current projects are. If you are asked to, ask sharp questions about the company and explain why you are the right person for this great job. Speak well. Be alert. Look refreshed and know how to cover up your mistakes without offending the company interviewer and making you look bad.

<u>Interview outer must be as follows</u>
1. Wear a crisp dark brown, dark blue or black outfit
2. Be fresh! Do not party the night before your interview
3. Get to the interview location at least one half hour before the interview
4. Relax. Study the company mission statement before the interview
5. Spot-check your hair. Look professional, speak well, bring your best game
6. Make sure you present with at least two copies of your resume in a fresh binder
7. Smile throughout the introduction and interview session
8. Say one nice thing, i.e., "nice suit" to interviewer. Everyone likes a compliment
9. Congratulations from me to you for getting the job

Carol D. Mitchell

<u>You are intrinsically sharp & savvy</u>

[Answer all questions honestly, and briefly
[Point out desires for timed growth in the company
    [Include all relative work experience
[Keep answers relative to the posted position
    [Be yourself; but don't go overboard
        [Use sound judgment
    [Prepare and present great references
      [Highlight problem solving skills
      [If you have been fired, don't lie
[Be honest, show growth and responsibility
[Turn trick questions into positive answers
[Be positive and spontaneous to all questions

Your Rights

Employment Guide

CHAPTER 20
In the News

Some lawyers have effectively, convinced employers that employees have but few rights when it comes to their job. Do not be bamboozled when it comes to your rights on the job. The documented cases below show that perseverance can produce great dividends for the employee who is serious about holding employers to oblige and respect their protected classes and rights under varying, specific employment law. Keep abreast of fighters who are holding employers accountable for their wrong actions and take heed to these winning stories.

<u>Wal-Mart Sexually Harassed Fight Back</u>

Source: Aaron Bernstein, BusinessWeek: (2005, March 11).

Subject: Corporate America may have stumbled on a break in fighting off employment class actions. They are watching closely as Wal-Mart tries to prevail in a sexual discrimination case that will be put before the U.S. Ninth Circuit Court of Appeals. This is a class action suit that

Carol D. Mitchell

challenges an examination of how the charges could slam Wal-Mart's constitutional rights to the tune of 1.5 million former female employees.

Backgrounds please come back on time

Source: Linda Coady, FindLaw: (2005, March 1).

A California appellate court has decided that if the employer wants to get nosy and investigate suspicious conduct on you, they have to give the goods to the employee with all the public records they dig up. The definitive statement here is: (drum roll please). "The employer must provide info to the employee *"within a reasonable time"*.

Under an issue of first impression the state's Investigative Consumer Reporting Agencies Act, Plaintiff Gene Moran was hired April 3, 2003, as a paralegal at Murtaugh, Miller, Meyer & Nelson. A computer search revealed that Moran had felony convictions. Moran was asked to resign on April 9, 2003. Moran files an employment discrimination suit in violation of the Fair Employment and Housing Act, violation of the Investigative Consumer Reporting Agencies Act, and infliction of emotional distress.

Somebody is blowing that whistle again

Source: Associated Press, *FindLaw*

The U.S. Supreme Court will hear whistleblower retaliation case to determine whether a whistleblower prosecutor can sue his former employers for retaliation after he reported a

Your Rights
Employment Guide

possible wrongdoing by the sheriff's office.

Is the scope of the First Amendment, which protects government workers from discharge if their conduct involves a "public concern" rather than personal, job related issues relevant? Alternatively, is this case really a question of personal concern or public concern?
The ninth U.S. Circuit Court of Appeals ruled that Ceballos' speech was constitutionally protected and the district attorney's office lost this one! Will they strike out in the Supreme Court? Stay tuned.

Now that's what I'm Talkin' About
Source: Sanchez, G. *Monterey Herald, (2005, January 28).*
Jury verdict in favor of plaintiff in sexual harassment and retaliation case.

A smart Fresno jury upheld the maligned employee who said she was raped and sexually harassed by her supervisor. It took six weeks for the civil jury to find Harris Farms liable for the sexual harassment and retaliation against a brave female Mexican worker who had worked in the fields for the Company for about fifteen years.

Sovereignty vs. Civil Rights
Source: Kober, D. *Sacramento Bee, (2005, January 27).*

Carol D. Mitchell

A class action lawsuit against Indian casino claims sexual harassment, age & sex discrimination, and wrongful termination. The question of sovereignty, by the casino against the seven plaintiffs, could make this case a must see procedure. The defendant's contention that its status as a sovereign nation nullifies them from most state and federal anti-discrimination laws is very interesting.

The Clock runs out for State Farm Insurance
Girion, L. (2005, January 11). *The Los Angeles Times*
When State farm cheated 2,600 claims adjusters out of overtime I will bet that the last thing they ever expected was for employees to fight them to an end of winning a $135 million settlement. Let's suffice this case to say, "your hand-sheet can

be worth millions to you." Just keep on being the great employee that you are and keep your good old calculator very close to your fingertips when working for rife companies like this one.

One Janitor, three chains and a hook on wages.
Source: Greenhouse, S. (2004, December 7.). New York Times

Three immigrant janitors prove there is gold in them there mountains when supermarkets try to sell you dishonesty in wages. Three happy janitors are now singing to the tune of $22.4 million dollars in a settlement that was reached in this class-action wage and hour lawsuit.

Your Rights

Employment Guide

April 7, 2004

Nina D. Rightful
2567 EarthLink Road
Detroit, Michigan 90000

<u>SETTLEMENT LETTER</u>

Dear Ms. Rightful:

This is to confirm our telephone conversation of March 21, 2004. I appreciate your telephone call in which you explained your concerns regarding your experience while employed by the XYZ Company and that you wish to receive a letter, RATHER THAN MONETARY COMPENSATION from XYZ Company that speaks to the need to ensure that the laws prohibiting discrimination are being followed at XYZ.

XYZ is committed to maintaining a workforce which includes the demographic groups reflected in the general population encompassing the differences in race, ethnicity, sex, religion and the myriad of other demographic characteristics. Concomitant with that diversity is the XYZ's clearly understood responsibility to adhere to its policies and labor contracts contain nondiscrimination

Carol D. Mitchell

policies in accordance with State and Federal law. XYZ conducts workshops and training classes for the purpose of educating its population about its responsibilities to manage its operation in a nondiscriminatory manner. XYZ undertakes affirmative action for minorities and women, for person with disabilities and for specified covered veterans.

The departments where you were assigned to work *are aware of the concerns you raised*, but understand the need to be *vigilant in ensuring that XYZ Company's nondiscrimination policy obligations are followed*. XYZ will continue to work to meet its responsibilities including the fair and nondiscriminatory implementation of policies and procedures in compliance with applicable laws and regulations.

Your Rights

Employment Guide

We very much appreciate the compliments given to Ms. Donna Madina and her efforts to assist you as well as those physicians who you reported so ably attended to your medical condition.

I wish you the best of luck in your new endeavor and again thank you for the opportunity to discuss your concerns with you.

Sincerely,

John Doe, Coordinator
Labor and Employee Relations

JD:lc

Carol D. Mitchell

Top Ten Jobs

RESOURCE: http://www.thinkadvisor.com/2014/05/06/top-10-best-jobs-of-the-future-2014?page_all=1

1. **Health Specialties Professor**
10-year growth projection: 36.1%
Annual salary range: $55,340 to $138,070
Total number of U.S. workers: 163,850
Typical education: doctoral or professional degree
Stress score: 51.9

2. **Financial Advisor**
10-year growth projection: 27.0%
Annual salary range: $49,410 to $124,680
Total number of U.S. workers: 183,420
Typical education: bachelor's degree
Stress score: 51.7

3. **App Developer**
10-year growth projection: 22.8%
Annual salary range: $72,290 to $116,630
Total number of U.S. workers: 643,830
Typical education: bachelor's degree
Stress score: 46.4

Your Rights

Employment Guide

4. Information Security Analyst
10-year growth projection: 36.5%
Annual salary range: $67,120 to $113,100
Total number of U.S. workers: 78,020
Typical education: bachelor's degree
Stress score: 50.1

5. Management Consultant
10-year growth projection: 18.6%
Annual salary range: $59,360 to $106,950
Total number of U.S. workers: 567,840
Typical education: bachelor's degree
Stress score: 47.9

6. Civil Engineer
10-year growth projection: 19.7%
Annual salary range: $63,850 to $101,660
Total number of U.S. workers: 262,170
Typical education: bachelor's degree
Stress score: 51.0

7. Physical Therapist
10-year growth projection: 36.0%
Annual salary range: $67,700 to $93,820
Total number of U.S. workers: 195,670
Typical education: professional or doctoral degree
Stress score: 54.0

Carol D. Mitchell

8. **Dental Hygienist**
10-year growth projection: 33.3%
Annual salary range: $59,600 to $85,310
Total number of U.S. workers: 192,330
Typical education: associate's degree
Stress score: 55.7

9. **Market Research Analyst**
10-year growth projection: 31.6%
Annual salary range: $44,110 to $85,310
Total number of U.S. workers: 430,350
Typical education: bachelor's degree
Stress score: 45.8

10. **Brickmason**
10-year growth projection: 35.5%
Annual salary range: $35,860 to $62,810
Total number of U.S. workers: 58,730
Typical education: high school diploma
Stress score: 46.2

Your Rights

Employment Guide

Top Staffing Agencies

(1) AD Personnel
(310) 284-3939
1180 S Beverly Dr # 715
Los Angeles, CA 90035
Areas Served: Santa Monica CA, Beverly Hills CA, Los Angeles CA, West LA CA, Long Beach CA ...

(2) Select Personnel
(562) 944-4110
10730 Patterson Pl
Santa Fe Springs, CA 90670
Areas Served: Los Angeles CA, West Hollywood CA, West Los Angeles CA, Long Beach CA ...

(3) Labor Ready Inc
(562) 432-3521
116 W 7th St
Long Beach, CA 90813
Areas Served: Glendale CA, Long Beach CA, West LA CA, West Los Angeles CA, Culver City CA

(4) MJO Staffing Inc
(562) 699-1230
11205 Washington Blvd
Whittier, CA 90606
Areas Served: Santa Monica CA, Long Beach CA, Gardena CA, Los Angeles CA, Whittier CA ...

Carol D. Mitchell

(5) AMR Staffing Services
(562) 432-3101
2401 E Pacific Coast Hwy
Wilmington, CA 90744
Areas Served: Long Beach CA, Wilmington CA, Carson CA, Torrance CA, Los Angeles CA

(6) Reliable Resources Inc
(323) 722-1318
5254 Pomona Blvd
Los Angeles, CA 90022
Areas Served: Beverly Hills CA, Culver City CA, Los Angeles CA, Glendale CA, Long Beach CA ...

(7) Tri State Staffing
(310) 521-9616
450 Westmont Dr
San Pedro, CA 90731
Areas Served: Long Beach CA, Culver City CA, Los Angeles CA, West LA CA, Beverly Hills CA ...

(8) Act 1 Staffing
(310) 750-3400
1999 W 190th St
Torrance, CA 90504
Areas Served: Long Beach CA, Torrance CA, Los Angeles CA, Carson CA, Culver City CA ...

Your Rights

Employment Guide

"Final Message to Readers"

American workers have effectively served this Country well for centuries. Consequently, we are easily led by conscience to hurry into another job before claiming that which is rightfully ours from the old Company that let us go. If a Company feels puissant enough to let you go easily; you must find your endurance to fight them and guard your good name. Your work record is life-long. So turn around, take care of your business, and preserve your work record before running into another job.

Never blame yourself for being methodically and uniformly fired. Today's workforce is subjective and intractable enough for anyone to be fired or replaced at a moment's notice. I know that because it has happened to me before. As an aging working professional, I have managed three large companies. In those jobs, my duties required me to work with employees from a variety of beautiful national cultures. The most difficult thing I ever had to do on a job was let someone go, but, I was always proud to see workers stand up to large companies and to me, to defend their employment rights.

Caught up in the capitalistic goals of businesses and

Carol D. Mitchell

mergers in the free world, commerce competitiveness here and abroad bred an aggressive industry with exceptional opportunities for vast and expansive growth. However, I have watched firsthand the use for older workers diminish significantly in this Country to a point we were woefully forced out of old industry, as new and younger workers came into our jobs to handle new core concepts inside an ever-changing, complicated technological boom in the American workplace. The augmentation of computers and automation, eliminated many jobs in short notice and corporations got avaricious enough to ask for a cut of some workers hard earned benefits and to my dismay some courts granted such request. Consequently, as a growing number of American workers find themselves fired or laid off and replaced by youngsters, computers and automation, this incalculable informational handbook will make it much easier for all workers to defend their rights, and hard earned benefits in the American workplace.

Your Rights
Employment Guide

When you are being fired, the process is carried out in an intricate, and well organized routine that is predicated usually on rigid boardroom demands or numbers that were crunched by people who did not visually see your great contributions to their business or industry. Corporate decisions generally are final and leave no room for job resumption for the exiting employee. Firing such workers got depressing enough for me not to want to fire people anymore. I saw fewer exiting employees who challenged these corporate decisions. I got worried. I watched helpless as many of them left behind valuable employment earnings and assets to rush responsibly and sometimes un-responsibly into another job.

Those words being said, there are still many great companies in operation that believes in their employees, and you may just be working for one of them. Constantly observe the changes in your company today and on a regular basis.

Carol D. Mitchell

It is key for you to understand your *"Employment Offer Letter."* Be prepared for transition by viewing and acknowledging the real possibilities of change.

I wrote this book for you, America's greatest asset! If you did not get what you deserved in your last job, use the knowledge that you gain from this handbook to bargain next time for a better working contract. Ask an employment law attorney to review your new or old employment contract and help you negotiate for benefits that you deserve. You are a gem. Your strong work experience is priceless and you should get paid for your educational value and all of your work life experiences. I encourage you to protect yourself. Keep this employment informational guide at your easy dispense and utilize this manual to find out about important and meaningful aspects of how to preserve your longevity in today's American workforce and much more. I dedicate this book to America's working class employees. I hope that I have been able to help you understand your work rights better. May all that this book contain assist you and yours for many years to come. Good Luck!

    Here is thanking you in advance for reading this book and here is wishing you the best in all of your professional and private pursuits in life!

Your Rights

Employment Guide

BIBLIOGRAPHY

"**50 Standard interview Questions.**" (2003, July 15.) *College Grad. Com.*
Great interview questions for employees

"**100 Best Companies to Work for in America.**" (2005, January 1.) *Great Place to Work Institute.*
Comprehensive guide to shift out right companies to work for.

Alston Jr., & Taubman G. (2005). *"Union Discipline and Employee Rights." Google search*
Comprehensive resource for union members.

Associated Press, *Findlaw.* (2005, February 28.) High Court to address Whistle Blower suit." Article: "Legal Matters re: Employee Rights that is in the News." Pp. 1-2.
Current legal decisions.

Bernstein, A. (2005, March 11). *"California Legal Matters." Article:*
"Legal Matters re: Employee Rights that is in the News." Pp. 1-2.
Useful inspirational Information for fighters of labor rights.

"**California Consumer Rights.**" *(2005, February 25.) Chamber of Commerce.*

Coady, L. *(2005, March 1). I "Employee must get background check Records in Reasonable Time."*
FindLaw. For employees who want to know background check rights.

"**Communications Workers of America vs. Beck.**" (1998). *487 U.S. 735, 108 S. C. p. 2641.*

Carol D. Mitchell

Department of Employment & Fair Housing. (2002, November 1.) *Right-to-Sue Instructions," DFEH- 300-03. (2003, January 1.) Pp. 1-3*

EDD – Employment Development Department. (2003, October 1.) "California Programs for the Unemployed." Periodical: Pp. 1-22. Resource for the fired or laid-off employee, etc.

"Employment Harassment Policy." *(2004, November 1.).* *Http://www.equalrights.org/pulications/kyt/temporary/.as Great educational tool for women.*

"FedEx Service Information, FedEx U.S. Package/Envelope Services." *(1995 -2005). FedEx. Resourceful information for times and rates.*

Hayes, G. *(2005). I "My Business," Pala media limited.*

Hedding, J. *(2005, May 16.). "Best Places to Work: Pp. 1-4.* Http://phoenixabout.com/cs/bestjobs/abestplaces2004.html

Korber, D. and Magagnini. *(2005, January 27.). "Harassment Suit Targets Casino, Sacramento Bee* "*Legal Matters re: Employee Rights that is in the News." Pp. 1-2*

"Largest Temporary Employment Agencies." *(2005, February 5.). Boston Business Journal.* *The five largest temporary agencies in the world.*

"Microsoft Word 2002 Quick Reference Summary." *(2002).* *(Computer Program) Redmond, WA.* Microsoft Corporation. Shortcut cheat sheet, (for college graduates, or every day American workers.).

"Required Posters for the Workplace." (2005, January 1.). *California Chamber of Commerce.* Informational guide required postings for the American Worker.

Your Rights

Employment Guide

Sanchez, G. (2005, January 28.). *"Farm Workers Case Draws Mixed Reactions."*
"Legal Matters re: Employee Rights that is in the News." Pp. 1-2
"State of California Department of Industrial Relations – Division of Labor Standards." *(2001, May 1.). Filing a Claim.*
Tarbell, S., B., *Administrative and Executive Assistant, 2nd Edition. (2002.). Learning Express, LLC.*
"The 21st Century Workplace: What Employers look for." *(2005, March 12.). University of Technology Sydney.* Great prep. Resource Material.

"United States Postal Service. Shipping Products & Services." (1999 – 2005).
Quick reference guide for employees.

Wagner, R.F. (1935). "Election at Ford Motor Company River Rouge Plant, *Dearborn, Mi.* NLRB
Introduction: *First Sixty Years."* Historical – NLRB.

"Workers Compensation in California." (2005, February 26.).
Http://home.earthlink.net/ssblaw/wcinfo.html
Smart chart for employees.

Carol D. Mitchell

ABOUT THE AUTHOR

2011 award winning writer, Carol Denise Mitchell, was born at 8:30 A.M., on May 12, 1955. Mitchell, sixth of sixteen children, is the daughter of Zebbie Thomas Charles, Sr., and Tasceaie Carise Charles. Mitchell was reared in Los Angeles, California, during the noteworthy era of the Civil Rights Movement, and she recalls how living in Watts, California, during this era in American history, was a motivating influence behind her writing career.

"I remember the Watts Riot, when the city imploded for three long, life-changing days. Encouraged by my mother; I knew this kind of degradation and Urban ruin, was not going to be remedied fast enough for the kind of changes the community deserved. One year after the riots, we moved thirty-five miles east to Pomona, California," says Mitchell. She concludes that being a living witness to an infamous part of Watts history left an indelible imprint on her wanting to be a part of change that helped her old community via writing and memorializing such events first-hand.

In 1977, Mitchell moved to the Northern, California, Bay Area, to launch an impressive thirty-year writing career. She wrote What Happened to Suzy winning praise; and, a coveted (2011) book award, for its' message of healing and hope.

www.ingramcontent.com/pod-product-compliance
Lightning Source LLC
Chambersburg PA
CBHW051648170526
45167CB00001B/379